KENNETH P. NOLAN

A Streetwise Guide to Litigation

Jack —

Hope you enjoy your career
as much as _I_ did. Work
hard, keep your integrity
and don't forget to laugh!

Ken

 **Section of Litigation**
AMERICAN BAR ASSOCIATION

Cover design by Jill Tedhams/ABA Publishing.

Library of Congress Cataloging-in-Publication Data
Nolan, Kenneth P.
A Streetwise Guide to Litigation / by Ken Nolan.
    p. cm.
    Includes bibliographical references and index.
    ISBN 978-1-61438-755-8 (alk. paper)
    1. Lawyers—United States—Biography. 2. Practice of law—United States. I. Title.
KF373.N59N65 2012
340.092—dc23[B]   2012039406

http://www.ShopABA.org

To Nancy
with love

Contents

Introduction

The law is a wonderful profession. It is also demanding and stressful, with much hard work. Many times I wanted to quit and return to teaching high school with weekends and summers free. But after 35 years I still enjoy it. It's exasperating at times, always challenging, and requires a multitude of talents—speaking, writing, researching, analyzing, advocating, and dealing with people—some good, many horrible. It is stimulating and rewarding. I recommend it.

I have handled all types of litigation—from small claims court to megamillion-dollar lawsuits. I have tried a wide variety of cases: auto, slip-and-falls, medical malpractice, aviation, products, construction, and contract disputes—in state and federal court. I've litigated throughout the country—Cleveland, Chicago, Miami, Buffalo, Lexington, New York, New Jersey, Connecticut, and Ohio. I've written appellate briefs and argued appeals. I've won and I've lost. I've made plenty of mistakes. I still do. We all do, even the famous ones—the ones knighted by the media or by themselves as *Super Lawyers*.

Over the years I've written about my experiences in *Litigation Journal*, published by the Section of Litigation of the American Bar Association. My inspiration was never some mysterious muse, but ordinary people, those I grew up with and lived with on those hard, wonderful Brooklyn streets. Where getting knocked down or losing was celebrated as character building. Where games were played dodging cars or in barren concrete schoolyards. Where homes, schools, and churches were crowded and everyone knew everyone. It certainly was excellent preparation for interacting with lawyers, judges, clerks, and clients. Not being raised in a leafy suburb was a blessing, I suppose.

A few years after I started at Speiser Krause, Paul Rheingold, a superb lawyer, suggested I submit my name to *Litigation,* since they were searching for editors with journalism experience, which I had from working at *The New York Times.* I started as an associate editor in 1982 and have been with *Litigation* and the Section of Litigation ever since. I now write the "Sidebar" column and am a senior editor.

My work with *Litigation* has brought only joy and fulfillment. And it allowed me to write—not as much as I should have, but periodically. My articles—collected in this book—are not about country club living or the philosophy of a celebrated Supreme Court justice. It's not the stuff you were taught in law school, but how to survive and succeed. I hope you like it and find it helpful. If not, regift it.

I have many people to thank for encouraging me. From Speiser, Krause, Nolan & Granito: Gerry Lear, Frank Granito, Jr., and his son Frank Granito III, Jeanne O'Grady, and Christina Fry—all wonderful friends and great lawyers whose wisdom and good humor make working a joy. The firm's founders, the late Stu Speiser and Chuck Krause, brilliant lawyers who gave me an opportunity and always supported me. Because of these people and others—Dave Hernandez, Ursula Campbell, Dia Ramos—I never left the firm and never will.

My *Litigation* family. I joined bar associations to drum up business. That occasionally occurred, but the real advantage was making lifelong friends, probably my first real friends who weren't from Brooklyn. People like Mark Neubauer, Larry Vilardo, Chris Lutz, Judge Jeffrey Cole, Gary Sasso, Ambassador Howard Gutman, Kevin Abel, Will Park, Jim McElhaney, Steve Miller, Chuck Tobin, Rob Shapiro, Jake Stein, the late Peter Baird, Judge Bob Gettleman, Steve Good, the late Bob Aitken, Marilyn Aitken, Judge Joe Greenaway, Pam Menaker, Maria Rodriguez, Robin West, Judge Elaine Bucklo, Edna Epstein, Lee Stapleton, Jean Snyder, Bill Pannill, Doug Connah, the late Charlie Wilson, and so many other editors and staff who publish the best legal magazine in the world. Also kudos to the Section of Litigation for supporting our editorial board in times good and bad. The Section and its members should be proud that for decades *Litigation* has published timely, engaging articles by accomplished authors accompanied by humorous and poignant art. All without ads.

Particular gratitude to my good friend Chris Lutz, who shepherded this book to publication by editing it and advocating its merits. Chris is thoughtful, wise, and measured—admirable qualities, all of which I am lacking. In addition, Chris is terrific fun, with a sharp, dry wit. He spent innumerable hours reading each word, suggesting changes, all of which improved each article. Not only do I value his guidance, but I am honored that he would spend his valuable time on this project. Many, many thanks, Chris.

I also acknowledge my good friends Fred and Kathy Hills, whose experience and expertise in the publishing world provided sage and needed advice.

The luckiest day of my life was when I met a 17-year-old Nancy Cirrito outside of O'Keefe's Bar on Court Street. I followed my father's advice—don't you lose that girl—and we're married for 39 years. The smartest and happiest decision I ever made. We have four amazing children, two of whom are lawyers. Kenny and his lovely wife, Jessica, have blessed us with our grandson, Luke. Our daughters, Caitlin, Lizzy, and Claire, are intelligent, beautiful, and so much fun. They only tell me I'm annoying once a day. I thank them for always making me laugh and always making me proud.

Nancy has given me love, guidance, and understanding. And she makes me happy. I'm a very lucky guy. Thanks, Nance. Here's to 39 more years together.

Kenneth P. Nolan
Brooklyn

Part One

Opening Thoughts

The Basics

I always wanted to be a world-class athlete, able to throw the Mariano fastball, do a so-very-quick crossover dribble leaving my opponent looking like a chump, knock down a tailback with a shrug of my broad shoulder. Instead, I was born a hottie. Yeah, those are my daughters laughing in the background; but what do they know, they think George Clooney and Bradley Cooper are cute. If you're reading this, you're probably somewhat like me—ordinary for the most part, gifted not really, proficient if we're being kind.

I'm a trial lawyer. Even though my photograph has yet to adorn the cover of *Vanity Fair,* I'm pretty good at what I do. And what I do is work—mundane, often tedious work. A lot of it—weekends, nights, and rushing down the gum-stained, slick subway steps, briefcase in hand, silently cursing the old geezer in front who clutches the worn-smooth handrail and moves fearfully. Hurrying because I'm late or because I want to be early. Just hurrying because that's what I do. What most of us do. And we do it all day long.

It's hard and laborious; and as I age—er, become more experienced—I realize it's the ordinary work that makes you good, makes you win, makes you successful. Not always fun but, heck, what job is fun anyway? I guess if you're Julia Roberts or Tom Brady, life's not so bad. You're better looking than everyone else and your headache is to sign a few autographs.

It's the same with trial work: not movie-star glamorous but easier than running into a flaming tenement with 50 pounds of gear and a hose heavy with water. It's mostly just monotonous. Yet there are moments—yes, they exist—when you connect with the jurors and see them unconsciously nodding as they lean forward during your closing, knowing that your wonderful words have convinced, have soared through the fog to the endless clear sky. The unshaven mailman is focused, listening, agreeing. He's with you in this place, and your simple but beautiful language has transformed this pedestrian dispute into the American ideal of justice. You yearn to preserve this moment—the captivated faces, your voice that glides through the drab courtroom, the failed nonchalance of your adversary. The court clerk has stopped reading the box scores, and the tired, jaded judge has stopped doodling and peers over her weathered reading glasses. Sadly, there is no James Boswell or Ansel Adams to preserve the moment. But you will always remember and strive to replicate this scene.

And you did it alone. You were the one who persuaded. The shy seventh grader who spoke so quietly and quickly in class is now so eloquent with her deep, dark eyes and poised, determined voice. These same words, once so nervously murmured, have become a force, psalm-like, and the jurors are believers, ready to sing *Amen,* to vote for your client.

Yes, there are such moments, whether before a jury or a skeptical judge, whether with a bet-the-company case or a needless discovery motion. The substance is unimportant. It is the feeling, the exhilaration. You have to seize such moments, savor them when the radio alarm blasts at five a.m., and you're too tired to stumble to the shower for another day of pressure-filled, mind-wearying work. These slices of triumph exist and, even though the world does not watch, they are worth the effort and pain. These are the reasons you became a lawyer, a trial lawyer. But how do you get there?

My CYO basketball coach used to whine, "You can't teach height," as he stared at our team of shrimps. Yao Ming was in the NBA because, after all, he's just a bit taller than everyone else. Others are born with beauty, intelligence, or artistic inspiration—Mozart, Raphael, Beyoncé. Law, of course, is more pedestrian. Sure, there's talent involved, and the greats were (and are) gifted as orators, writers, analyzers. But most of the stuff we do can be learned. It's not that hard.

You can learn to write, to research, to speak. Read books, take a course, attend bar association lectures, listen to the old-timer who shuffles down the hall, *The Wall Street Journal* in his trembling hand, recounting the strategies and successes of cases big and small yet all long forgotten. Pretend law is golf, and practice, practice, practice. Hear your piano teacher's sarcastic voice as she orders you to do it again and again until you get it right. Even Edward Bennett Williams used to rehearse his anecdotes. With hard work you can be better. You can grow, you can improve, you can be good.

But first put your ego in your purse. So you passed the bar and graduated from ivy-covered universities with majestic oaks filtering the sun. Maybe your Aunt Diane was impressed, but a jury doesn't care. You passed the bar by memorizing a bunch of mostly useless garbage. So stop trying to be so cool. You're a young punk who has to learn the fundamentals. It takes time, nights when all your old college buddies are in some Irish joint on the Upper East Side, having a few, laughing, trying to collect e-mail addresses. And you have to do it on weekends and early mornings and holidays. It's work, after all. Not fun, but dull, plodding work. And it's difficult is to admit you're 27 and know nothing. Get over it.

Do what I did. For an oral argument, create a detailed outline and practice, just like in high school speech class. In front of a mirror and out loud. Continue to practice the next day in the car or on the subway whispering like a derelict crackhead. Confidence is the key. If you aren't panicking, you can think clearly and respond coherently. Don't be afraid to check your notes, to read the quote from the controlling case as you argue. You're not graded on style but on substance.

The day of my first jury trial, I was waiting in the hall for the judge when I looked across at two veteran lawyers trying a nonjury matrimonial case. Because I was so inexperienced that I didn't even know where to stand when questioning—no lecterns in state court—I popped into the courtroom for a peek. I figured seeing how the pros did it would give me confidence. It was enlightening. Every other statement from these skilled lawyers was "urn, er, withdrawn Your Honor" or "strike that." Where's the eloquence, the rhythm? I could do this, I thought. So can you. Don't worry; you're never as good or as bad as you think or fear.

Writing, too, improves with hard work. This is probably the toughest challenge, especially because so many schools prefer the "grammar and spelling don't count" philosophy. But if Mrs. Lynch can teach me and 50 other third grade knuckleheads penmanship, grammar, and the *Baltimore Catechism,* you can learn to write simple declarative sentences. Please, please stop the lawreviewese. Drop the *hereins,* the *heretofores,* and other legal mumbo jumbo. Just write in short, clear sentences. You don't have to be Hemingway, but write a draft and then reread and edit it.

Have someone who learned to diagram a sentence, who has heard of a gerund, read your work for syntax and clarity. If a sentence runs on and on, cut it in half. This is hard work, for spelling, punctuation, and grammar are thought of as antiquated in this immediate and informal age of the Internet. Leave your e-mail abbreviations and style on your smart phones. In your legal writing, be concise and coherent. And while you're at it, read *Eats, Shoots and Leaves* by Lynne Truss. It's time you knew how to use an apostrophe.

When I first began practicing, I was amazed that I knew more about the facts and the law of my cases than many of my more senior adversaries did. Lawyers were reading the file as they waited to argue a motion, searching for a summary of the facts, not understanding medical procedures or how products work. Unless you are a junior lawyer in a prosecutor's office, there's really no excuse for this. It's easy to spot, and it shows. Even at depositions, these attorneys are oblivious to the errors of their clients because they had never visited the scene or learned how to read an EKG.

I once tried a medical malpractice case for a client whose physician perforated his heart during a myocardial biopsy. Sounds easy, right? The defense attorney, however, was more than prepared. He put on scrubs and attended such a procedure, spending the day observing, questioning, understanding. He knew as much as the surgeons, and more than me. I won, but he tried a terrific case, showing the jury the instruments, educating them on how thin the heart wall is, beating up my expert. He was so convincing that the miserable judge reduced the verdict.

That's what you have to do, too—go to the factory, meet with witnesses, eyeball the experts. Not only must you obtain hands-on knowledge, but you also must use the Internet to gather biographical and other data. Google everyone and everything. Facebook, LinkedIn, Twitter. and other social media reveal details about parties and witnesses. The Net, however, is no substitute for personal meetings and interviews. A photograph cannot replace the knowledge gained from visiting the scene, touching the instruments, understanding the mechanics. A telephone conversation provides sound, not how the person looks or dresses or how he'll sell at a deposition or trial. So dirty your hands; do it yourself and immediately, before the rain washes away the skidmarks, construction changes the road, the bare branches erupt with green.

Ask questions. Millions of them. Like everyone my age, I've forgotten what I didn't know. So don't be afraid to ask the dumb question that reveals your ignorance. It takes guts, but you only have to ask once and then think of a comeback when you're kidded later. My daughter called from college in a panic when she lost her wallet and had no money. My wife's simple response was to tell her to go to the bank and withdraw some. Because my daughter had only used ATMs, she had no idea that you could actually withdraw money without a bank card. The most obvious is easily overlooked.

Know more than the experts or the judge. It's the only way. In one aviation trial where my client, Mrs. D, survived a plane crash but was severely injured, the defense attorney slyly asked his medical expert on redirect, "Didn't Dr. A write in his records that Mrs. D was too emotional about illness." Answer: "Yes." "No further questions, your Honor." Because I had nearly memorized all my client's medical records, I was able on recross to show that this comment came in a medical note eight years before the crash and was referring to her *mother's* illness *not* her own. Without these facts at my fingertips, the jury may have assumed that my client was a nut case who exaggerated her injuries. There's plenty of downtime during most trials, so spend it working and rereading depositions and medical records, not talking loudly in the hall.

Law is not all fun and games. Many hate it. When my son started law school, a good friend, a lawyer, seriously asked, "Why would you let him go to law school?" Like I was some child abuser. Recently, three young lawyers I know left the profession—didn't like it. No other prospects, just "See ya later." Too much work, too boring, no time for anything else. It's tough to say goodbye to a three-year-old with a fever and run off to argue a motion on the number of subsections in the interrogatories.

One young associate asked me whether, after practicing for more than 25 years, I was happy. My candid response was, "I don't know, I never thought about it." Yeah, it's a frightening response; I'm sure I would be Exhibit A at some clinical psychologists' convention. So don't wait 25 years before you ask yourself this question. (By the way, my answer now is "Yes, relatively.")

Litigation is a sacrifice, and to succeed, you must devote time and effort. I taught high school English for five years at John Jay, a tough Brooklyn high school. Not easy with disrespectful, illiterate kids and chaotic halls, but it was 180 days a year, six hours and 20 minutes a day; we had summers off. Of course, the older teachers who knew more Joyce or Faulkner than any of my college professors pushed me into law. They always believed I made the correct choice—but I'm not so sure come July when I'm sandwiched on the 4 train between two guys whose last showers were taken during the Bush administration.

Don't be like the callous co-op board at 927 Fifth Avenue who destroyed the nest of Pale Male, the red-tailed hawk, and his mate, Lola. They were evicted after 11 years and 23 offspring because the pompous rich folks didn't want the minor inconvenience of these lovely birds. Even after the nest was rebuilt, the lesson was apparent—money can't buy class.

Periodically, I'm forwarded an e-mail that records some obnoxious behavior by a cursing, ill-mannered attorney. Most of these blowhards are frauds. The toughest guys in my neighborhood were the quiet ones who would just smack you silly and never say a word. Screaming expletives does not mean toughness, although I've been known to give in to that temptation. Courtesy and civility are ideal responses even in the face of rudeness and ignorance. I recently read where an attorney barked at a deposition. It's tempting to want to put a leash around his neck, but much more effective to be professional and win in the courtroom, rather than in the conference room.

Or use humor, as one Dallas lawyer did when his adversary moved for document production returnable on Christmas Eve although the lawyer had written the court advising that he would be going away that day with his family for Christmas. His response to the Grinch was with a Seuss-like poem. That his adversary would move to strike his vacation letter and request such a hearing on Christmas Eve is why our profession provides material for stand-up comedians. It's time we stopped the pettiness, the infantile behavior. Richardson Lynn, dean of John Marshall Law School, reminded me that the late Frank Rothman advised, "Never file a motion when you can write a letter. Never write a letter when you can make a phone call."

In your heart and your head, you must care. If you do, you'll be kind and considerate. And if you don't know or remember how, attend one of the training sessions at the large firms, which teaches etiquette so their attorneys, young and old, will realize that lateness is wrong, checking a smart phone during a meeting is rude, and saying *please* and *thank you* is appreciated.

Clarence taught George in *It's a Wonderful Life* that life is precious even though you don't always realize it. So it is with law: It's rewarding if done properly. You will learn that life is short, so make it a satisfying, enjoyable one not only for yourself but for others. After all, you're a lawyer in America. "God shed His grace on thee," as Ray Charles, Kate Smith, and so many others sang and knew.

To Young Lawyers

I never wanted to pick up fetid garbage in the sweltering sun. Or tiptoe on iron 40 stories in the air. Or get the finger after I ticketed some yoyo doing 80 on the BQE. Instead, I taught high school English to tough, listless teens. Then I attended law school at night because I needed credits above my bachelor's to maintain my teaching license. Of course, it wasn't until I finished my first semester that I learned that the Board of Education wouldn't accept law credits for licensing purposes. Had I checked, I would never have entered law school, become a lawyer, or been called the f-word by a federal judge.

After screaming at bored bureaucrats about the unfairness, I almost quit law school but was convinced to continue by a fellow teacher and other veterans at John Jay High School whose insight into literature and life was unique. This experience of not determining whether law school credits would satisfy my teacher requirement taught me the magic formula for a successful career—check the facts and be nice to clerks.

My son became a lawyer because his college roommate's dad told him, "I don't care if you sell pencils on the corner, Kenny, go to law school. It's a great education." And it is. Expensive, too. Well, not when I attended (luckily), but now it is for sure. My daughter has graduated from law school but, unlike my son and me, she has always wanted to be a lawyer, I think. As a member of the mock trial team in high school, she crossed witnesses in the courtrooms of the Southern District of New York. She and her classmates were poised, intelligent, and clear. In high school, I could barely complete a sentence. Especially in front of a girl.

Now she and her classmates have graduated, taken the bar, and entered the big, bad world of law where even the Supreme Court gets dissed by the President. So I figure now is when I can bestow the wisdom of my many years, the knowledge and guidance I never had except from those weary high school teachers. I can supply a road map to a thriving, rewarding, happy career. It exists, doesn't it?

Get a job. That's not easy today, especially with constant layoffs and jobs as scarce as an adjournment in the rocket docket. As friends remind me, it wasn't easy for us, either. Having our kids struggle and work like pack mules is good for them, my Brooklyn buddies growl. Builds character. "You want sympathy," my mother would snap if one of us didn't make the team, "look it up in the dictionary."

And now that white-shoe firm you dreamt of since you were six is not hiring. In-house jobs have evaporated faster than the value of my 401(k). Your life, so carefully planned, is a mess. OMG. Well, swallow your pride and take what you can get. Times will improve.

If you're shut out of the legal biz, use your talents elsewhere. Of course, that's easy for me to say after practicing for decades. And not getting hired is painful, especially if you yearn to try cases, do deals, argue appeals. "Adversity is only an opportunity to grow," Jim Baron, former basketball coach at Rhode Island, teaches. Don't sit around praying for the perfect position. Do something, anything. It won't kill you. You may stumble into a career that will make you content, even happy.

Don't Regret Law School

I know, I know. Most graduates are in hock to their eyebrows. Why law school tuition is so outrageous is a subject for another day. If I were in my mid-20s with a mountain of debt and few job prospects, I would be cursing my delusional decision to attend law school. But 30 years from now, you'll be glad you went.

Remember the counsel that my son received from his roommate's father—something rarely mentioned in this era where the sole motivation is the almighty buck: law school can be a great general education. You learned to read and think and speak, and, if you're really lucky, to write. Sure, you had to survive first-semester boot camp and ivory-tower professors whose only contact with the real world is their daily commute. And you learned about how the world works, which you probably didn't know before. But, except for that silly bar exam, it's in the past. And you're better for it. Well, mostly.

You don't have to practice. Knowledge of law and the legal system gives you an advantage others lack. Many CEOs are lawyers, as are stay-at-home moms, chefs, artists, firefighters. Not so long ago, a good friend's dad passed away, a longshoreman on the Brooklyn docks. You want to know what it was like, he told his grandchildren, watch *On the Waterfront*. He made sure his kids had options other than that kind of life—that they studied and learned so they wouldn't have to break their backs to buy bread. Law provides alternatives. You can use muscles, mind, or both.

Remember, too, that you don't know it all. It is difficult for a baby lawyer to recognize limitations. Sure, strive to learn different areas, but you can't master everything. I recently received a phone call from an experienced attorney who was representing a French domiciliary who was injured on an international flight. He tried to settle the claim but couldn't, and then started the action in the local federal court. Only one problem: Pursuant to treaty, jurisdiction is not in the U.S. but abroad. Defendant's motion to dismiss was made after the statute had run. Moral: Ask for help, early and often.

Seek the knowledge of white-haired fogies. Sure, she might give the "What are you, an idiot?" look. So what? You'd rather screw up? Whether in a gastropub or the office, don't advise unless you're absolutely sure. "You probably have a case, but consult someone who does this stuff every day. I'll e-mail you some names. Call them." Don't be a hero.

Be honest. Sometimes it's difficult. It's easy to tell a client and your partners that you're going to win and kick some plaintiff butt. It's much harder to report that the case is problematic, flawed; we might get hit big time. But bringing bad news is your job, too—to analyze, provide guidance. Don't sugarcoat. Tell the truth, both good and bad. Do that in your papers, too. Too many lawyers ignore harmful precedent, distort facts, or exaggerate the impact of a favorable decision. A savvy judge will spot the charade and never believe a word again. Admit weakness and then distinguish it.

And stop pretending you're Superwoman. Learn to say "No." "I don't have time to take on this assignment and complete it this evening. Two other projects will keep me here til daybreak. . . . No, I really don't understand what you want, can you go over it again?" The grouchy senior lawyer who's asked you to do these chores can be exasperating to talk to, and he won't necessarily want to hear what you have to say—but you have to say it.

I belong to a neighborhood bar association that does good work—it holds monthly CLEs, collects toys at Christmas for the soldiers at Fort Hamilton Army Base, has occasional cocktail parties where young lawyers mingle with judges. Yet every few years another member is indicted, usually for stealing from escrow or some other sacrosanct account. All good people, I thought—people I know and trust. Never in a million years would I believe it. The story is the same: "Others have the four-bedroom home, three cars. I deserve it." The temptations to stray from honesty will be everywhere.

It can happen to you. Just read the blogs: insider trading, looting an estate, bribing ambulance personnel or a judge. All to live a bogus lifestyle. I grew up in what now seems a very strange world. If you couldn't afford a baseball mitt, a car, a house—guess what?— you didn't buy it. Who doesn't want to be one of those hedge-fund guys with the private jet, Monets in the living room, mansion in the Hamptons? But many are caught and disgraced. If you want to gaze at water lilies, move to the sticks.

Be yourself. You're impressive, with enviable qualities both academically and socially. You even sound like Sinatra—but only to those who have had three or more shots. Don't try to be someone else. If you're slow and methodical, fine. It's okay that you're not as eloquent as Barack. Determine what's effective—for you. You have distinctive and valuable strengths. Use them.

Initially, you will believe that everyone is so knowledgeable, accomplished, and all more than you. After 30-plus years, even I know a little law. With a dose of experience, you will realize that you're just as bright and capable. Preparation and attention to detail breed success.

Don't be a phony. John Edwards, successful trial lawyer, wanted to be President. Except he didn't like people. "I know I'm the people's senator, but do I have to hang out with them?" he was quoted as saying by a former aide. Sure, you can fool some, but eventually they'll whisper, "See that guy? He's a rat. Don't believe a word he says."

It's a great life. It is. The law blogs are littered with complaints: tedious research, long hours, layoffs. Stop whining. Nothing's perfect. Not even my golf game. I've enjoyed my career—frustrating at times, but intellectually stimulating. Every now and then I've helped some person or family when they're desperate. Law has taken me to the Red Hook projects and the Champs-Élysées. I've handled cases before mostly fair, considerate, pleasant judges. I've litigated against clever yet principled adversaries, whose word is gold. I've met amazing people, now friends, from Buffalo, Los Angeles, Chicago, Tampa, Lexington, Honduras, Scotland, and Italy.

Yes, you'll wake in the silence staring at the ceiling as your mind races. You'll smart from the occasional elbow to your kisser. You'll lose. Everyone does. But you're a better person having survived law school. You're joining a valued and essential profession. With a touch of hard work, you'll support yourself, a family. You will laugh and occasionally weep. But you'll have fun. A lot.

Getting Business

So you wanna be a big shot, make the big bucks, have your mug on the cover of *Time* magazine. Or maybe, just maybe, your dream is different—a polite practice, help a few widows and orphans, earn just enough to afford pre-pre-K tuition. To do either, you need the Holy Grail—clients.

I know they're pains, demanding this, asking for that, changing minds, complaining about fees, expenses, driving you batty with irrational ideas. But without them, you starve, your house gets foreclosed, and your kids whine day and night that they'll have to limit their texts to 1,000 a month.

If *Utopia* allowed lawyers, the most accomplished would make the millions, garner the accolades, and be revered on the blogs. But this is the law biz where job security, as they say in *The Sopranos*, is commensurate with the amount of money in the last envelope handed to The Boss.

At one time, thoughtful, reserved attorneys, those who sat silently in offices contemplating strategy until an ingenious plan was created, were as highly valued as the guy whose sister-in-law was CEO of Exxon. But no more, not in this economy, not in this profession, which reveres profits over performance.

At noisy brunches on gentrified Smith Street in Brooklyn, we trumpet art, principle, and love over the dollar, but occasionally when we pass a just-renovated brownstone, the ache of jealousy becomes palpable. Man, would I love to live on those polished parquet floors with the mahogany chair rails and original lion-clawed tub. Oh, well, maybe someday, you tell yourself, knowing that the someday may never happen.

Making it happen isn't easy. When I was admitted to the bar, I stopped wearing jeans. I discarded my pathetic attempt at the shabby but cool look, opting for an image of a classy professional, the one to seek for sage advice. Even weekends: When work was finished, my friends would lounge in their tattered duds. Not me. I'd be strutting around in pressed chinos and collared shirts. The nerd look. It never worked, of course, but I instinctively knew that you should start from day one cultivating clients, whether it was Mrs. Murphy down the block or the local candy store owner.

What always amazes me is that others—skillful, conscientious lawyers—didn't know this. They don't seem to know you need clients to pay rent, experts, staff. "I'm brilliant" was the illusion. "Everyone knows that, and so clients will come a-knocking at my door." Because I always thought I was a bit dumb, I never believed my baby blues would earn me a living. "No one's giving you nothin'" was my neighborhood's refrain. If you want something, my mother lectured, get it yourself.

This "It's a tough world out there" reality comes as a shock to those 20-somethings or 30-somethings who've sailed through life. Then the economy tanked and those high-paying, secure jobs evaporated like so much of our confidence in the American dream. Now you have to hustle, scratch, and claw just to buy pita.

Millions are great lawyers—insightful, diligent, even eloquent. Yet to be secure when firms merge or liquidate, and when lawyers jump from firm to firm in search of, what else, more money, you need clients. Without them, you're a worker bee—replaceable. With them, you're a contender; you're somebody.

Yes, it's work to acquire and develop clients. After you finish the brief, answer 92 e-mails, stuff your bag with a week's reading, there's still that boring community meeting about the traffic light. Doing the business development rounds is humbling for sure. Kissing the local politico's ring, becoming involved in alumni or local bar associations, or having dinner with a young assistant general counsel. Of course, you're special and everyone should recognize it. But they won't if you don't work at it.

Make contacts, meet people, and follow up. The first President Bush was renowned for sending handwritten notes—nice to meet you and all that. Back then, writing those notes took time. How difficult is it to shoot off a text or an e-mail? "A pleasure. If you ever need any legal assistance, let me know. I'd be glad to help."

You don't have to plaster your smarmy mug on ads in the A train next to those for hemorrhoid relief. But you have to let people know who you are and what you do—whether it's corporate, criminal, or real estate. Whenever someone tells me, "I didn't know you did med-mal work. I thought you only did aviation," I feel like a failure: I wasn't clear about my work or what our firm did. It's not hard; it just takes motivation and effort.

In addition, you have to look and act professional. I'm always dismayed when another lawyer doesn't have a business card. "I just ran out" is the feeble excuse. She can't be interested in new business, I conclude. And if she's too disorganized to carry a simple card, I figure, she'll probably miss a statute of limitations or some other deadline.

My ex-partner, Larry Goldhirsch, used to preach that you should always wear good suits and drive an expensive car. Clients want their attorneys to be successful. There's some truth to this, although I never got the gold Rolex thing. After a client retained us, one forwarding attorney said, "It didn't hurt that you drove a Mercedes." I didn't want to tell him that, until I finally splurged, my last three cars were minivans.

Suits are reserved only for court these days, but don't dress like a slob. Stash a decent jacket in your office in case the General Counsel wants you to buy lunch at The Four Seasons. Delete the embarrassing photos on Facebook. Just as you immediately Google and Facebook the cutie you just met in McSorley's, corporate clients do the same. Sure, everyone plays beer pong and gets trashed, but the world doesn't have to see you bent over a toilet bowl.

Have attractive, professional promotional material—a brochure, a website, stationery. Did I read that even Cravath hired a few more public relations people? Heck, if Cravath needs assistance in reminding corporations of the quality of their work, so do you. In a subdued, classy way, of course.

Check your e-mails, letters, and briefs for typos, misspellings, and grammatical mistakes. Your written work is a reflection of your competence. It is a continual, and virtually permanent, advertisement for who you are. If your written work is sloppy or replete with errors, those reading it will think you are an idiot. The days of "It doesn't matter if you win as long as you have fun" are over. It's your job to get it right.

Meet people. Make use of organizations—bar, community, political, social. Become involved in something you enjoy. You may not become outside counsel for Apple by volunteering for the local nonprofit, but you never know what contacts you'll make. And you might help others.

The young are more resistant to old-fashioned networking than my generation is. I've been involved with the American Bar Association and with its publications since 1982. I've made great friends, had many a laugh, and was even referred a case now and again. Yes, there's a trade-off. When you're at a meeting, you're not home with your spouse and children. It's a tough choice, very tough, and if it's not for you, I respect your decision. There's nothing wrong with choosing family over career.

Keep in touch. I'm still friendly with guys I knew in first grade, kids I played basketball with in the schoolyard, my many cousins. I thought everyone knew the nicknames of scores of playmates. I finally realized these lifelong close relationships were the exception. At a recent cocktail party, one entrepreneur introduced his building manager for his million-square-foot properties. "I grew up with Andy," he mentioned. Andy is qualified, no doubt, but it didn't hurt that they lived on the same street. My buds are not billionaires, but they refer their co-workers and relatives, which is a compliment indeed.

Don't be a phony about it, but stay in contact with those you like, whether sorority sisters or high school co-conspirators. It's easy with Facebook and other social media.

Stand out. I'm amazed at my children and their friends. Smart, beautiful, conscientious, fun. But maybe a bit spoiled, too. One was laid off after two years of working diligently. "I can't believe this. I put in my time," he wailed. He was learning that it's a challenging, competitive world.

These new lawyers are better in all respects than my generation is. But there are millions of similar overachievers. Be different. Acquire a skill that distinguishes you—fluent in Korean, experienced in health care, able to write a simple declaratory sentence. Have a superlative. Develop something that gives you pleasure. It can't hurt.

Lecture and write. So many opportunities, so many blogs. An article like this might be mentioned in foreign places such as Illinois or Canada. And my day is made when I receive an e-mail from Medicine Hat or Saskatchewan commenting on something I've written. Turn your ever-so-boring research into a thoughtful article. Some blog will publish it and some big-time Ivy League–educated lawyer will read it and not know any better. Suddenly, you're an expert.

Elbow your way onto a CLE panel. Aren't there thousands of programs daily? Once you do one, you'll realize that all these gray hairs (like me) on panels are fairly ordinary. A bit like pulling the curtain on the Wizard of Oz—and maybe you can be a wizard, too.

The ease of getting and keeping a job has disappeared—at least temporarily. Realize that law is big business with all the arrogance and callousness of British Petroleum. Once you're no longer essential, it's thanks for all the hard work, now get out. The simple way to remain indispensable is to be like Hyman Roth—always make money for your partners.

The Courthouse

When you first march into a courthouse—be it a tiny, battered bandbox with worn, scarred tables and squeaking juror chairs, or a majestic new federal one with carved, gleaming benches and plush dark carpets, you never know whether you will find justice and integrity, or whether you'll be home-jobbed, your arguments scorned, your case deep-sixed.

Yes, courthouses are strange places, secular churches really, built to inspire awe and reverence with priests in black vestments looking down on the masses. The walls are lined with paintings of somber saints, and on the altar sit implements of power—a gavel and tomes which contain the Gospel according to Congress. Sinners stand before these judges and plead their cases. They confess and beg forgiveness. Penance is dispensed publicly and sternly in fines or years, and, of course, you must obey.

For some lawyers and clients, it is an alien place to be avoided, since only bad can result. For others, it is a nurturing home, a den where disputes are resolved equitably, where the cold statue of Lady Justice comes alive and justice is dispensed with wisdom and common sense.

As with any other adventure, you rarely know what awaits you when you climb the stone steps and pass through the metal detector. The reasons for uncertainty range from the facts to the law, to the venue, to your expertise. But there are human factors that are also important. For these American-established churches, like similar places of worship in Rome or Jerusalem or Mecca, are comprised of people, learned and magnificent, flawed and foolish. And it is not only your interaction with Her Honor that can determine success, but with the other acolytes—the law clerk, secretary, court officer, calendar clerk. They are the essential yet often silent pieces of the judicial puzzle who run the courthouse, who read the endless motions, schedule the cases, and shepherd the jurors in the elusive quest to capture justice.

Occasionally the pieces fit, and the system works. The judge struggles with her rulings yet applies the law to the facts without worrying who is rewarded or harmed. The foreman in the clean white shirt and scuffed shoes proudly rises to announce the verdict as the other jurors watch him speak their words. The courtroom is quiet, the jaded court officer and clerk respectfully gaze at American democracy in action. And whether you win or lose, you got your fair shake. It didn't matter if you were yellow or brown, Muslim or Hindu, rich or dirt poor. You came, tried your case, and a verdict was announced. That's all you're entitled to, all you can ask for. Now take your blow-ups and other exhibits and get lost. There's another case in the hall, and around here we spit them out, two a week or more.

This is what we lawyers worked and hoped for—to participate in a trial where justice prevails, and everything is decided on the merits. This is why we spent months studying arcane legal decisions, memorizing deposition testimony, and interviewing witnesses—so we could skillfully represent the client, introduce evidence, and make arguments to convince the jury and the court that we're right and should win.

Yet, as we all realize, we live in a flawed world. It is a place of petty and evil people. And the courthouse is a microcosm of this fragile globe. As litigators, we deal with people. It's not easy. Check out the anonymous postings in Rants and Raves on Craigslist, and you will read hatred, ignorance, and cruelty. All types inhabit any busy courthouse: Most are good, but all are everyday people with their own grudges and prejudices. Some work there, including those bright lights that passed the bar. You're no different, even though some believe that a framed sheepskin on the wall excuses rudeness and arrogance.

So here are some ideas that may help you win the case, make partner, be a star, or, more importantly, obtain an adjournment.

Be respectful—to everyone. Newsflash: Most people in the courthouse aren't in love with lawyers. Heck, most of our families don't approve of half of what we do. So what? That's the other guy, the one who sued Benihana in the "death by flying shrimp" case, as the New York tabloids termed it. The chef tossed a shrimp at a patron who tried to dodge it, injured his neck, and tragically died 11 months later. The jury quickly tossed the $16 million case amid the newspaper jokes and editorials. That's not me or you, although I have a few cases which bark when I open the file.

But while you may believe you'd never go that far, there's a bit of arrogance, stupidity, and rudeness in us all. Despite my best efforts, one or more of these can suddenly appear like that creature in the movie *Alien*. I'm standing in line at court, waiting patiently, when the clerk decides it's time for coffee and leaves. Or some pushy regular jumps to the front to ask a question which results in a computer search, and back and forth, and you're late for your appearance, and your face gets red. Just as another question is asked, that ugly, terrible creature jumps out of your body and says, "What's going on here? There's a line, and you should wait your turn. How come you're helping him and not the next person in line? Moron." And then the clerk fixes you with a cold, disgusted stare, and when you are at the head of the line, he decides to take his time, so you're there twice as long. Then he finds a minor error in your papers that means you have to go back to the office, redo them, and return tomorrow.

Put yourself in the clerk's position. He's civil service, which means no Christmas bonus, even if he works his tail off. He's sitting at his ancient, cigarette-stained metal desk, with paper piled high, obsolete computers that break down, and a line out the door that never ends. Half the lawyers don't know the court rules even though they're simple and available. The clerk's job is to make sure you've done your job, so all day he sits there and explains why you screwed up, why your papers don't comply with the law. "You have to do them over again, can't accept them, check Section 1493(a)(2). It wouldn't be fair, can't let you take advantage of your adversary, sorry."

Here's a helpful rule of thumb: Assume that all who work in the courthouse are professionals who are as intelligent, refined, and well mannered as you.

Where I was raised, the vista of what you could be was limited. Our Greatest Generation parents were depression-raised, immigrant-based. With a bunch of snot-nosed brats, the concern was food and clothing, not the quality of the dorm rooms at Stanford. We learned to work young and hard, delivering papers, shoveling snow, painting fences, walking up tenement stairs hauling boxes of groceries. Safe, secure jobs were paramount. While in college, I worked part-time for *The New York Times,* and whenever I told a neighborhood guy what I did, the response was always, "Mailers?" "No." "Printers?" He assumed I was in a union rather than on the editorial side.

So we became cops and firefighters, nurses and teachers, construction workers. Sure, some gravitated to Wall Street, law, or medicine, and there was the occasional priest. There were many success stories, but there was little correlation between brains and career. Many who opted for civil-service jobs were more intelligent, more accomplished than those who pursued college and grad school.

That is true within the court system. Court clerks and officers are often as sophisticated as those who try cases. They should be treated as such. Sure, they didn't go to Princeton or Duke, but many are college-educated, doing essential and effective work. And even if they're not, treat them with respect. "Please" and "Thank you" are effective and mandatory.

Realize who has the power in the courthouse. I selected a jury in a medical malpractice failure-to-diagnose-lung-cancer case and was sent to a trial part to open. My adversary made a last-minute motion for an evidentiary hearing to determine if the X-ray we intended to use was the one given by his defendant doctor to my client and later read by another physician whose notes indicated a mass in the left lobe. The defense attorney made claims of fraud and spoliation. While the judge was checking his calendar to schedule the hearing, the court clerk immediately announced, "Judge, you can't do that. You're a trial part. We try cases here, Counselor.

We don't have evidentiary hearings. If you want a hearing, go back to Judge Smith [the assignment judge]."

The judge, who had a bright disposition and kind manner, agreed and said he would hear argument on the motion to hold an evidentiary hearing tomorrow morning, deny the motion, and begin trial. That evening, settlement negotiations progressed, and after the judge officially denied the motion, the case settled. Thanks to the clerk.

Judges are human—for the most part. Every day, they work with the same people—a law clerk or two, a secretary, a court clerk, a stenographer, a court officer—all of whom have an interest in what goes on in the courtroom. Law clerks, from the Supreme Court of the United States to the County Court in Onondaga County, research the law, summarize the facts, and draft opinions. When I was in law school, I interned for a criminal court judge who had an issue involving whether the search and seizure which uncovered a handgun was legal. This was my first assignment and I had only taken the basic criminal law class, so I spent the weekend in the library researching until I stumbled upon the answer. The gun had to be tossed, much to the chagrin of my judge. Nonetheless, she did so, even reading part of my memo verbatim into the record.

Busy trial judges do not have the time to read the endless paper they receive, research every issue, and write learned, succinct opinions. They have to rely on others for assistance. It's not a question of effort but of time. So you have 25-year-olds analyzing everything from minor discovery disputes to momentous constitutional issues. This process isn't ideal, but it happens, and you can't ignore it.

Get to know the clerks, court officers, and the like for two reasons: It can't hurt, and they're generally nice people. If you have to run to another courtroom, they can make sure you're case isn't marked off the calendar, or they can sneak you in early for a conference. Small favors, indeed, but crucial when you have four cases with different judges.

There's a family-style Italian restaurant a few blocks from my home. I occasionally stop by and grab a plate of orecchiette with sausage to go. One evening, I notice a local lawyer holding court at a table groaning with food. "Hey, Kenny," he calls, "you know these guys," introducing me to various court officers, clerks, stenographers. I mention a case or two, recall a favor, and nod knowingly to the lawyer who's much shrewder than I thought. He won't win a case by stuffing them with veal rollatini and broccoli rabe, but 90 percent of our work is motions, conferences, and discovery disputes that are scheduled and sometimes decided by these same people—and so his hospitality can't hurt.

Golfing with the judge or having a beer with the court officer won't guarantee success. "Kenny, I just don't wanna get hurt," reasoned one old pro. You still have to convince the jury, and nothing beats expertise and four aces. Six or 12 ordinary citizens decide whether you win or lose, but judges have tremendous influence over jurors. Some take over questioning—like the judge trying a stairway slip-and-fall who questioned the plaintiff who had testified that the stairway was dark and dim. The judge asked if she could read a newspaper with the available light in the stairway. When the plaintiff responded "No," the judge continued in front of the jury, "And yet you walked down the steps?" It was obvious to the jury what the judge thought of the plaintiff's case. Be aware of the judge's tendencies during trial and plan accordingly.

Sure, you can win even though the judge doesn't like you. Sometimes it's part of the underdog strategy, but it's much easier if you get along. I once tried a case for about six weeks in a tiny courtroom, and for that entire time the judge never said a single good morning to me or my clients. He hated me, my clients, and my case, and even though I won, it was a miserable experience. Every day was a battle against my adversary *and* the court. It was a horrible time. Know whether this is likely before you open.

The more you know, the more skilled you are. And it's often the little things that determine victory. Jurors try hard to decide the case on the facts only, but we know that perception is often reality. Which is why we dress to please, why one lawyer changed wedding bands for a trial because he thought his real wedding band was too gaudy, and why we soften accents when we try cases away from our home area. Tone down that Texas twang if you're trying a case in New Jersey.

Use the manners that your mother taught. Make her proud by treating all in the courthouse with respect and good humor.

Part Two

Handling a Case

Judge or Jury?

Of course you want a jury: the sympathetic Joes who will intently listen during your opening, dismiss with contempt your adversary's hired gun, cry real tears during your masterful closing, and award you Lotto numbers in a verdict, making you rich, famous, and the subject of a cover profile in *The ABA Journal*.

Of course you hate juries. You represent the oil conglomerate that inadvertently spilled just a bit of an all-natural hydrocarbon on a beach no one ever used. Your client employs thousands, feeds and clothes families, but only a judge understands. She's seen it before and will not yield to the phony plight of the damaged. Any award she makes will be reasonable, somewhere in the ballpark.

In the parochial Brooklyn neighborhood where I was raised, stereotypes were not seriously questioned. You were called politically incorrect names. You were where your family emigrated from—good and bad. Behavior was explained by ethnic group. Education and exposure changed that perception but did not eradicate it. For instance, when I married Nancy Cirrito, the seating at the wedding was easy. Her family was near the buffet, while mine was near the bar.

It is the same for law. Stereotypes and received wisdom (or what passes for wisdom) persist: In civil cases, plaintiffs want juries; defendants do not. In criminal cases, the prosecution wants reliable

Judge Conservative; the defense needs to convince only one of 12 to be successful. Yet, like my childhood stereotypes, if these bromides are accepted without thought, mistakes will be made, people insulted (though no one complained at my wedding), and cases lost.

The decision of whether you try your case to a judge or a jury is often difficult and dangerous. "Good ol' boy" Judge Country Club may surprise you and slap your client with a decision that is disastrous and nearly impossible to overturn. And that sympathetic juror may be more callous than anticipated and remark, as one did to me, "You know, Mr. Nolan, I wanted to vote for you. But if your client says he was going 40 miles per hour, he was really going 60. I know. I've been there myself."

Usually, there really is no decision to make. As the plaintiff, you are more comfortable with a jury, and the plaintiff has the right to decide. But consider the consequences of your choice before routinely submitting a jury demand. And when you certify ready for trial, reexamine your decision. You may be able to stipulate to a bench trial if that's in your interest.

Judges are supposed to be immune from sympathy, to be fair seekers of truth. But some judges—and not just a few—are bitter and callous, incapable of providing equal treatment. Jurors react emotionally, but usually they try to do what they believe is right. The more you know about judges and jurors, the better your choice.

Therefore, know your judge and jury. Do your homework. Know your jurisdiction. Is it a typical suburban, home-owning, taxpaying venue? Conservatives do not give away the courthouse for a whiplash injury. But if your case is somewhat unusual, involving the environment, for example, what are their feelings? Do they care more about the logger trying to feed his family or the polluted lakes and streams? Do juries in your venue have a strong history of independence? The traditional stereotypes may not apply. To rely on them is to risk a fatal error.

Study previous jury results. Speak to lawyers who try cases daily. Stroll into shops, malls, diners, and eavesdrop. What newspapers are read? What TV shows are watched? Who did they vote for—Republican or Democrat? Who are the local elected officials, and what issues were decisive in their campaigns? Is crime the overriding concern, or the economy? The schools? Read the bumper stickers and local newspapers to obtain a flavor of your potential jury. It may shock you.

Hire professionals to survey attitudes and learn what the average Jane believes about issues in your case. If you are trying to a jury, ask the judge to allow jury questionnaires for potential jurors to complete in advance. Ask questions that not only relate to your case but also include work experience, union status, household income, political affiliation, and recreational activities. By reading these, you will gain a sense of the ideal or terrible juror.

In the mega-case, jury consultants are a must. But still use your own instincts. If you're an experienced trial lawyer, don't ignore your innate wisdom. You know if someone is wrong. Since you're trying the case, you decide. Don't cede that decision to another. If you don't feel comfortable, use a peremptory to boot off a troubling juror.

Know your judge. Research every opinion she has written. Learn her background, her educational pedigree, how she achieved her lofty position—politics or more politics? Who's her mentor? Speak to attorneys who have tried cases before her, her ex-clerks and court personnel. Does she sentence lightly or is she Maximum Sue? Judges have reputations, as plaintiff- or defense-oriented, pro-government or not. Search beyond the local gossip and examine each ruling; sometimes the reputation has little basis in reality. Judges evolve. What was once true may no longer be the case.

With knowledge of the composition of a potential jury and the judge scheduled to preside, you can make an intelligent choice. Obviously, you may not have a choice if your adversary has requested a jury or if the law requires a nonjury trial, as with the Federal Tort Claims Act.

Once you have gathered this information, analyze your facts. One white-collar criminal defense lawyer I know examines the type of crime, jury pool, and judge before deciding whether a jury trial is in his client's best interests.

If his client is accused of bank fraud involving millions, then these facts fail the smell test. It stinks. The chances of a jury acquittal are slim, especially if the defense is a complex legal argument involving subtle nuances of the law. The average juror will see only the millions and the elderly depositors cheated out of their life savings. A judge, however, may be better. He may accept the legal argument and hold his nose as he acquits the defendant. But be careful: Most federal judges are pro-government, often having been assistant U.S. attorneys.

In criminal cases, race can be a factor in the choice between jury and judge. A white cop accused of brutalizing a black person would be wise to consider having the judge decide his guilt in a jurisdiction where the majority of jurors are black. Jurors may have seen or experienced similar events, and any defense explanation would be scrutinized. For the same reason, a black defendant in an all-white area must also consider a bench trial.

Once the choice is nonjury, how is trial strategy different? One of my partners contends that a case should be tried essentially the same way, whether jury or nonjury. Do not assume a judge will shortcut the evidence or testimony.

Give an opening statement. The judge may interrupt you with questions. It is an opportunity to argue the issues or respond to the judge's concerns about your weaknesses. Let the judge tell you that she doesn't want a detailed direct examination of the credentials of an expert. Be flexible, but prepare your case thoroughly.

Educate your judge. Prepare a terse but direct trial brief on law and facts. If yours is a technical product-liability or securities case, submit a detailed brief explaining the product or procedure so that the judge can comprehend the facts. Within the brief, define terms; use illustrations, graphs, and photos. Set forth your contentions. Educate the judge in the most effective manner.

Another partner of mine, who practiced in Southern California, tells of a judge who was the trier of fact for a portion of a major wrongful death case, but who did not understand basic tort law. The lawyer had to cite *Prosser on Torts* to the judge, who kept repeating at sidebar, "It was an accident. He didn't mean it. That's not negligence." More than a month passed before the judge started to learn (or recall) first-year tort law and the reasonable-person standard.

Do not assume that the judge has experience in your specialty, no matter how simple. With the continued explosion of drugs and crime, many federal judges try only criminal cases. One remarked to me that he "hadn't tried a civil case in a year, and I'm just a glorified criminal court judge." Put law and facts in a brief that you constantly update as the case progresses.

In a nonjury case, evidence is treated differently. Juries love demonstrative evidence, elaborate video displays, colored charts, photos, and computer creations. Much of this appeals to the Facebook and MTV generations. Judges are impatient with demonstrative evidence that takes time. Video depositions will be ignored in a bench trial. The judge will read the transcript during halftime of the Cowboys game.

One Justice Department lawyer, who tries all his cases nonjury, warns that during a bench trial, the judge will want all deposition testimony submitted so he can read it later. Confusion can result since the deposition may be needed to lay a foundation of a yet-to-be-called live witness. Bring this to the judge's attention. Offer a summary of the testimony so the judge can follow your proof. Do not be intimidated by a judge who wants to race through trial and take shortcuts to the finish line. A logical presentation of proof is essential. Remind the judge of this.

My government lawyer friend also notes that in one case, the judge would hear no direct testimony of experts; instead, curricula vitae and written reports were admitted into evidence (much like the practice in many administrative agency proceedings). Before you open, study the judge's rules to determine his position on what testimony he will hear so you can be ready if an expected 10-day trial takes two. Prepare your expert for a truncated direct and an immediate cross.

The rules of evidence are often relaxed or even ignored in a nonjury trial. A judge will overrule the objection that the evidence is "inflammatory" or confusing. Hearsay objections are often disregarded. But make your objections anyway. Although the atmosphere in a bench trial is often more relaxed and informal, don't forget that there could well be an appeal. Make your record, by bowing and repeating in your best altar-boy voice over and again, "Just note my objection for the record, if Your Honor pleases."

Prepare your strategy knowing that what is inadmissible in a jury trial may either be admitted into evidence in a bench trial or at least seen by the judge before he excludes it. Amazingly, judges are human. They even have emotions (other than anger, which all trial lawyers have experienced). You cannot "unring a bell."

As one lawyer cautions, even inadmissible evidence may influence a judge. Of course, in the bare-knuckles school of trial practice, there are occasions when you can slip inadmissible evidence under a judge's nose before the inevitable objection is ruled on. Whether that's kosher, I'll leave to you and your minister.

Theatrics are muted in a bench trial. Judges are not swayed by some silver-tongued orator with a $200 Armani tie. Most prefer the Joe Friday approach—"The facts, Ma'am, just the facts." But a trial—even a bench trial—is part entertainment. Admittedly, judges need less than jurors, whose attention spans have a television commercial duration. But a judge's mind can wander, too: to the golf course, the vacation, or her grandchildren.

All agree that the judge takes a more active role when there is a bench trial. Witnesses should be warned to expect questions from the bench. If a question is omitted or is unclear, a judge will jump in, at times even taking over. Inquiries from a judge are a window into his thoughts. You never know what silent jurors are thinking, but, through questions or rulings, a judge will reveal her feelings.

After a vigorous and, I thought, devastating cross of a defendant's doctor, the elderly federal judge who had quietly sustained my adversary's objections peered over the bench and said sweetly: "You know, Mr. Nolan, if a jury was here, they would not have liked your raising your voice to the doctor." I realized what is effective to a jury can be counterproductive to a judge.

Now I have learned to probe in cross-examination. By his rulings, a judge will indicate just how far you can go, whether he wants an argumentative cross or a Joe Friday cross. In a nonjury trial under the Federal Tort Claims Act, the government had an expert in rehabilitation medicine testify. Since this physician had a congenital hip problem, she was in a wheelchair—in most cases, a very sympathetic and probably effective witness. You cannot verbally attack a witness in a wheelchair before a jury. This physician was obviously used to being treated with kid gloves.

During her direct testimony, she turned toward my client, Anna L., and spoke directly to her and her mother in a tone of a caring professional instead of a paid expert:

Witness: One of the things that comes up and I think it is real important that Anna and her mother understands this, Gloria (the translator) is not here to translate, can you translate for your mom?

The doctor then discussed how various drugs would affect Anna and which drugs would be better for her. All this time she continually looked at my client. I, of course, objected and the doctor retorted: " . . . I am a physician who cares very much about Anna's outcome." The judge remained silent.

The doctor continued testifying on direct, accusing me of ordering my client to dress shabbily:

Question: How did Ms. L present herself to you as far as her dress and the like?
Witness: I will take full responsibility for being concerned about that issue.
Question: Why is that?
Witness: Because Anna presented herself in a different way than she presented herself here in court. . . . She was very well dressed. She had on jeans, and I think she was wearing that jacket she has on today. And her hair was fixed, and she had makeup on and her hair was poofed up. And it made a difference in the way she looked. And I think she had taken the time to look pretty that day. I would be concerned about how she looks right now, if that means whether her depression has gotten worse or if she is not being permitted to dress up. I don't know.

I again objected to "these unsubstantiated attacks," but the judge remained aloof. This type of testimony continued concerning makeup to hide scarring:

Witness: I brought the makeup so Anna can have it. I don't know if Mr. Nolan would allow me to give her that.

I objected throughout, but politely and carefully. Then I began my cross. I started slowly and, as an experienced expert witness, she tried to answer questions with explanations. I decided enough was enough and I had to stop her:

Witness: No, you are wrong actually. And the reason you are wrong is because . . .

Me: Excuse me, Doctor.

Defense Counsel: Excuse me, she has a right to finish her answer. She is being cut off.

Judge: She wasn't asked the reason. And she volunteered a reason which was not asked of her.

Witness: Okay.

The judge's ruling was a revelation that maybe, just maybe, he did not appreciate her theatrics. After a few more questions, I sensed a slight break in her confidence, but there was still some resistance. I pushed a little harder, asking her a Yes/No question, which she answered:

Witness: Yes. And the reason—I would like to finish my statement.

Me: You can do it on redirect, Doctor.

Witness: I would like to answer you now. Is that okay?

Me: I would like you to answer my questions.

Defense Counsel: Your Honor, this is a bench trial.

Judge: Doctor, try to answer the question and try not to volunteer.

Witness: I would like to make sure the answer is complete. And he is not giving me an opportunity.

Judge: Defense Counsel can ask you anything he wants, but he is entitled to have an answer to the question he asks.

Witness: All right.

I knew I had won. I tore into her, firmly but with respect. I insisted on "Yes/No/I can't answer" answers. Without prompting, the judge insisted the doctor answer in that fashion. I was incredulous, and it was obvious that the judge enjoyed seeing this expert put in her place.

Outside the courthouse, the doctor told me bitterly and angrily in somewhat salty language that she had never been questioned like that. Moral: Listen to the judge's rulings. Through them, determine how far you can go. The trier of fact—judge or jury—influences all decisions throughout trial. Even the ultimate decision—verdict or settlement—is affected.

The world, of course, is not perfect. You win some you should lose, and at times you drag yourself to your office believing justice is dead, killed by a judge or jury too dumb for words. You vow to write that novel, so you can wave that million-dollar advance as you pack the photos of your kids and say *adios* to the pressure and inequalities of trial practice.

There are other times when the judge compliments you and screams at your opponent, and the jury smiles when they enter in the morning. Oh, if only all trials were like this one, you muse. Get that good judge or that good jury, and they will be. At least we can try.

How to Take a Deposition—Preparation

It's not your fault. It really isn't. As usual, we're to blame. After all, since birth we've scripted your lives with play dates, dance and tennis lessons, lacrosse and debate camps. If you didn't know how to do something, we'd hire someone to teach you. If you're no good at basketball or baseball, try hockey, soccer, golf, swimming—sports where suburban kids can excel. Failure was anathema. An 80 in biology? Hire a tutor, change classes or schools.

In P.S. 102 where my wife teaches, there's an Award Day at the end of the year. Great fun. Except now every student must receive an award. And teachers are not permitted to correct homework or tests with a red pen. Red ink must be really bad, as George Carlin would say.

"I'm not pickin' you. You stink!" Joe Kelly would scream as he looked some poor mug in the eye when we chose up for a stickball game. "The only reason we're letting you play is because it's your ball. You throw like a girl, you run like a retard, you can't catch." In the Brooklyn of my youth, you were told your faults—and to your face. Jackie Fats, Chubby Hopkins, Chin Grewshaw. And those were the nice nicknames. "Hey, Mrs. Nolan, could you lend me 10 bucks?" the local harmless ne'er-do-well asked my 87-year-old mother. "Cut your hair, Georgie, and get a job," was her immediate and loud response.

41

When the Knicks with Reed, Frazier, and DeBusschere won their championships in 1969 and 1971, the only coach was Red Holzman. Now every team has six. Tom Seaver had 231 complete games, my partner Frank Granito announced with amazement. Today, if a starter goes eight innings, it's champagne in the dugout.

It's the same with our work as lawyers. Used to be, "Hey kid, go pick a jury next Monday on this piece of crap. Learn something." Now we have jury consultants, eight associates organizing the file into neat categories on the computer, "with 27 8x10 color glossy photographs with circles and arrows and a paragraph on the back of each one," as Arlo Guthrie sang. It all impresses the heck out of the client and even the mediator who settles the case.

So we've become six-inning starters, yanked after 100 pitches, never setting foot in the courtroom. Sure, cases are tried, but only those dog cases, or where the rich guy's facing 20 and can't convince the prosecutor to offer less than a sawbuck. So we "litigate" our little fannies off, serving rogs and document requests, writing four-page indignant letters stuffed with mean, ugly, nasty language which then end, "With warmest regards." We make motions, have interminable phone conferences, and meet and confer until you want to toss your arrogant adversary and his bright yellow tie out the skyscraper window.

But, after 18 months of e-mailing hundreds of documents, depositions have finally been ordered. Five years after you passed that useless exercise called the bar exam, it's finally your turn. You're the lead. No more hiding; no more protective bubble. Just you. Others will be watching. You'll have to think and speak and decide—all at the same time. And if you screw up, word will slither out and you'll be embarrassed, hurt, humiliated, all the things we've desperately tried to prevent from happening in the modern conviction that failure is horrible, to be avoided.

With the dearth of trials, depositions have become more central, and crucial in some cases. When I first started, alpha litigators roared, "Wait til I get this phony SOB on the stand, I'll slaughter him!" Today, it's "Wait until you see my awesome motion for summary judgment, Dude." With my pasty-white skin, it's easy for me to wear a T-shirt that says "Pale is the new tan." With the change in trial work, I'm thinking of having one made that reads "Depositions are the new trials."

So here are my thoughts on how to prepare for a deposition.

No matter how facile or smooth, if you don't know your subject, the facts, you're immediately identified as a charlatan. Your adversary will slightly nod, turn toward the witness with a "Don't worry, he can't hurt you" look. So you must do your homework, sit for hours at your desk studying boring documents, learning the terminology of cardiac surgery, what causes an SUV to roll over, or how the subprime market doesn't work. And without that knowledge and effort, you will fail.

Determine Your Purpose

I'm sick of hearing lawyers screech how they're gonna destroy the witness, chop 'em up. Perhaps it's too many dreams of cappicola sandwiches and espresso at Satriale's. Those who howl the loudest have the least to say. They strut like peacocks, feathers abloom, and brag about how much they know, how proficient they are, how they've taken this deposition a million times.

"But what do you want from this guy?" I ask, and they look perplexed. For the first time, there's a touch of doubt. "Well, . . ." is the eventual response. And then they just blather on. They have no clue, never thought of it. Purpose is the first consideration. This may be the only time you question this witness, and you'd better understand why you are doing that in the first place. Let's face it; a trial is not happening that often.

Why are you taking this deposition? And what are you trying to achieve? Of course, I, too, mostly belong to the school of "Let's depose everyone, learn as much as possible, and sort it all out later." But before you send out 40 notices, consider whether this witness's testimony will enhance your strategy and help prove your case—or will she just bolster your adversary's position? You haven't helped your cause if the defense counsel can brag to the mediator or judge that you deposed 10 employees and each emphatically stated that his guy never forwarded an off-color e-mail, never mind sexually harassed anyone.

Analyze your goal before you notice the deposition, before you sit down to write your outline. Is this your one shot? Is the witness within the subpoena power of the court? Will he change jobs, move, retire? How does he help me? How can he hurt me? Treat almost every deposition as your only chance at the witness. Even if your adversary swears that he'll produce the witness at trial, nail it down on the record as tightly as possible. And your adversary's agreement to produce a witness at trial still doesn't mean much. People die, move, and fade into oblivion. And trial is a stretch anyway. Question the witness as if it's your only time. If you know his answers on some subjects will devastate your case, maybe you should avoid those lines of questioning. It can be a tough call, but that's why you make three times what a teacher earns.

Have an objective for each deposition. Plan and work to achieve that goal, whether it is to gather facts or learn the corporation's internal training mechanism. Have contingencies, so that if the witness veers into areas that you didn't want to cover, you'll have a strategy to explore that area or limit testimony.

Usually, I depose all those who actually witnessed the incident. What did you see, hear, say, write? You were at the corner of Maple and Main when the cars collided? Did you see them collide? Oh, you turned when you heard the bang. How far away? Did you speak to the drivers? Cops? Passengers? Other witnesses? Overhear anything? Take photos? See the damage? On and on, until you wring every bit of information, delineating between what the witness saw and what she believed happened.

An impartial witness is gold, as he has no allegiance to any party, making his testimony more credible. But make sure he's impartial—do you know anyone, ever meet them, speak to them, see them? Know their relatives, friends, acquaintances? Do your relatives, friends know Mr. Smith, Mrs. Smith, anyone in the Smith family, know any friend or acquaintance of the Smith family?

Ask hundreds of questions to find out what the witnesses know, how they know it. Facts and what people believe are facts are often different. Learn everything from a witness; you don't want to be shocked at trial or mediation when the testimony is, "Yeah, I heard the plaintiff mutter that she shouldn't have had that third dirty martini."

With such knowledge you can challenge your client's version—they don't always tell the truth, you know. Years ago, after I put the small settlement on the record in court, my client, who claimed his damaged arm rendered him essentially useless, turned and excitedly asked, "Does this mean I can go bowling tonight?"

So I depose every witness directly involved in the incident—for example, every nurse or doctor who treated the plantiff. You want to know what they did, saw, and heard. Whether you take the deposition of the physician in charge of the Department of Surgery or the head nurse—neither of whom was involved in the treatment of your client—is more nuanced. Then you have to evaluate whether these witnesses will help or hurt your case.

Based on your investigation, you know that some witnesses will testify adversely to your theory. Is it better to know before trial how damaging their testimony will be, or do you chance ignoring them, hoping they'll relocate to Myrtle Beach before trial? My predilection is to depose them so you know what you are facing and can minimize their testimony by raising issues of their versions of the facts during your questioning or through other witnesses at later depositions. Knowledge helps not only in valuation of your case but in preparation of your witnesses as well.

Other witnesses, those who are in the corporate chain, those who trained the negligent pilot, might be treated differently. If your goal is to stick the corporation with punitive damages, you may wish to limit the deposition to the inadequate training and the lax oversight of the company instead of focusing on the errors of the crew, especially if the pilot's actions were universally agreed to be negligent.

You may have to ascertain whether the negligent pilot had a reputation of not following procedure, but if you learn that the chief pilot had a terrific opinion of the pilot, don't make a record about what a great guy, husband, father, T-ball coach he was. Get what you need and let your adversary question or bring back the chief pilot in three years to proclaim the pilot's goodness.

It's a fine line, and sometimes you'll take your lumps as the well-prepared witness testifies with authority that the corporation's commitment to safety was the best in the industry. And you may even have to explore this response: How do you know it's the best?

Have you studied other safety procedures? How many? When? On and on until you identify the hyperbole and have him admit that he really didn't study the entire industry. And then you ask: "So you really don't know whether Corporation X's safety practices were better than Corporation Y's, do you?"

Take into account age, where the witness lives, and even pension information to determine if the witness is likely to be around at time of trial. Most are aching to sit in the sun and do nothing. Even if they're like me—live, work, and probably die within 10 miles of where they were born—the transcript will be used in mediation, settlement discussions. So you have to balance the knowledge you obtain from a deposition against the harm adverse testimony can cause in mediation, settlement, and eventually at trial, especially if there's a chance that the individual won't be able to be subpoenaed when trial rolls around.

It is axiomatic that you must know the facts, the subject, and the corporate procedures. Do the research, study the operating manual, search the web. Let's face it: we have to learn in a short time what the witness has been doing all his life. Think of *My Cousin Vinny* and Mona Lisa Vito (Marisa Tomei) on the stand as an expert. She was able to blow away the prosecutor because she knew 10 times what he did about cars. Like me, however, she knew nothing about grits.

Know the law, the burden of proof, and the jury instructions. Except for a few mom-and-pop shops, every corporation does business in many states and nations. So knowing the law is no longer that simple. Eventually the judge will determine which law, but until then, study all possibilities and prepare your questions accordingly.

Keep copies of the potential jury instructions and law on burden of proof in the file. Before every deposition, read them so you can tailor your strategy to what the judge will tell the jury. It's not that you'll try the case in the deposition, but that you'll focus on what's important legally.

If many different states or countries are involved, do a choice-of-law analysis. Research the judge's previous decisions for insight into how she will rule. Involve your partners, tell them your thoughts, and learn how you're wrong. Ask for help. You'll need it.

Nearly every case is met with a motion for summary judgment. Gather sufficient admissions and documentation through questioning to create issues of fact on key points. Any deposition has multiple purposes and uses. Take time to plan strategy before you enter the conference room. It isn't easy to explain to your partners and client that the case was dismissed because you failed to establish a fact or ask a question. "We'll appeal that horrible decision" are not the words that will bring you fame and fortune.

Use an outline. Of course you need one, and if you're really inexperienced, do what I did and write every question: What is your name? What is your home address? Sure, others at the deposition may ridicule you, but you're young and you'll get over it. Eventually, you'll graduate to an outline of topics that you'll explore and then check off as you complete them.

For many years, I kept the basic written questions handy and always reviewed them at breaks and just before I completed my questioning. Depositions are free-flowing. You never know where an answer to a simple question will lead. You have to follow the answer, and that can take you off the path you planned; a handy basic outline will remind you of points you haven't covered yet. "Doctor, has your license to practice medicine ever been suspended or revoked?" was a standard question with a usually standard answer until one day, the cardiologist answered "Yes." An hour later, after going where that "yes" led, I looked down at my outline and was back on track.

No one's memory is good enough to stay on track through every diversion. Without written words, you will forget (yes, even you), omitting topics and areas of importance. In fact, some savvy or ruthless adversaries will deliberately start fights, interrupt your questions, and make improper objections in an effort to disrupt your thinking, your line of questioning. You will be flustered or angry or amused, and your mind will wander. Words on paper make you return to your themes and strategy.

Organize your exhibits. Make a bunch of copies, enough for each attorney. Put them in separate folders, neatly labeled. Nothing is worse than to disrupt the flow of a deposition by having someone run to the copy machine or pass the document among all the lawyers because you only brought the original and a copy.

Be organized. Mark your copy so that you can easily and quickly focus on the portion you want the witness to read. "I show you Exhibit 12 and refer you to page three, paragraph two, the sentence beginning with the words . . . ." When you establish a rhythm in the deposition, the witness will answer more readily and sometimes more honestly. If you constantly have to break for copies or fumble around in your file for an exhibit, the witness has time to think and prepare an answer. And when you walk into a deposition with your outline and exhibits properly organized, others will respect you.

You may never be a Clarence Darrow or even a smooth-talking Bill Clinton type. But with diligence, preparation, and organization, you will win. And in litigation, style points don't count—winning does.

How to Take a Deposition—Execution

Don't try to impress me. It won't work. Sure you're brilliant and know all about the Federal Rules and the really important cases, probably even their citations. So what? So you're smarter than me and better-looking, too. Join the club. That's no big deal.

But this is a deposition. Just take it and shut up. If you're looking to impress, drag an unconscious kid from a burning building or join the Marines and kill terrorists. But if you're looking to build street cred, a deposition is not the place.

A deposition is the accumulation of information, not a trial. It works slowly, akin to a boxing match—jab, jab, jab, your left to his right eye. After a dep or two, a few land, most miss. Another dep and there's redness, slight swelling. Finally, after a few more, a small cut appears and eventually blood begins to trickle. He's weakened, can't see that well, tries to protect. You depose a few more witnesses, then the blood flows and you know you have him.

I've never seen a knockout at a deposition. Not even a TKO. Not even when Larry Goldhirsch asked the dentist who, in one sitting, yanked out 12 teeth of some poor woman:

"Doctor, are you a good dentist?"

"I'm the best dentist in the world," was the reply from a guy whose patient lapsed into a diabetic coma immediately after treatment.

49

Your job is to ask short, simple questions, and force the witness to tell you everything she knows. Compel her to reveal and identify documents. Obtain an admission or two. Do these and you've done your job. And I don't care if you're not eloquent, if you fumble and stumble with your questions. As long as you can gather the appropriate information, then I'll be impressed. How suavely you question, I don't care. Save the Perry Mason stuff for the courtroom. Just learn the facts—and realize that getting them may require slow, repetitive, precise inquiries that are just the opposite of suave and eloquent.

Remember: there's no such thing as a stupid question. If you don't know the answer, ask. Even if you do, ask. You may look like a moron, but so what. You should be used to it by now. Too many are worried about appearances rather than results. Ask away, look foolish, but insist on an answer. Don't assume you know the answer. If the purpose of the deposition is to learn what the witness knows, let the witness testify.

Make the witness define all terms, phrases, and words. Even simple ones.

"You testified that your company performed an internal investigation. What do you mean by *internal investigation?*"

Or even better, "When you use the words *internal investigation,* what do you mean by *internal?*" And then, "What do you mean by *investigation?*" And "Please define *internal investigation.*"

Note that in my initial question I used the term *internal investigation* twice. Many lawyers ask as follows: "You said that your company performed an internal investigation. What do you mean by that?" Sure, everyone probably understands *that* refers to *internal investigation.* But as was said in the movie *Casino,* why take the chance? Precision is best—even though it can be tedious.

Always repeat names and terms. I hate when lawyers ask:

"You spoke with Mrs. Gilbert?"

"Yes."

"What did she say?"

Better is "What did Mrs. Gilbert say?"

Besides ensuring there is no confusion, doing it this way makes excerpts of the transcript more usable with motions.

Forget pronouns. Toss them in the dump. Repeat the exact words. If you have to read the deposition at trial, the jury will never be confused as to who you meant when you used *she, him, that.* And the witness can never claim, "Well, when you said *he,* I thought you were talking about Mr. Alonzo. I guess I was confused."

> "Exhibit 24 mentions the phrase *flight training.* Do you see that phrase?"
>
> "Yes."
>
> "What does *flight training* mean?"

"Objection. He didn't write that document. The document speaks for itself." I never know if that objection is legitimate, but I always shove it aside by asking, "What is your understanding of the phrase *flight training* as contained in Exhibit 24?"

Every term of art must be defined by the witness. Almost all the time, the answer will be pro forma. But occasionally you'll be pleasantly surprised. And asking the witness to define a bunch of words or phrases will add some pressure and unease to the exercise. With such pressure, some witnesses begin to crack a bit and talk more, trying to please. The more the witness talks, the more you learn.

Ask one question at a time. Consider this monstrosity: "Can you tell me what you have done, if anything, to prepare for this deposition? Have you read any materials to prepare for this deposition?"

Two questions. If the answer is "Yes," you have no idea which question the deponent is answering or what she is saying. Go slowly, take your time. One by one. Simple and short are always best. It's not always possible, but try.

> "Can you tell me what you have done, if anything, to prepare for this deposition?"

Even this is terrible. If the deponent answers "Yes," then you have to follow up by asking, "What have you done, if anything, to prepare for this deposition?"

And what you may get is this answer: "Nothing."

Stop using "Can you tell me . . . ?" "Do you recall . . . ?" "Do you know . . . ?"

"What have you done, if anything, to prepare for this deposition?" With this question you should finally have an answer that means something. And, by the way, I've never known whether "if anything" adds anything. In fact, some would say it is a subtle encouragement to a witness to try to figure out how he can say that there *wasn't* anything. But I'm a lawyer and I have developed terrible habits. (I am proud to say that I have finally kicked the "hereinafter/heretofore" addiction.)

Another example:

"Do you recall if you had a conversation with Mr. Turner?"

"Yes."

"What did you discuss?"

"I didn't speak with him."

And then it takes 10 minutes to straighten out the mess. The problem is that the first question asks only if he "recalls" whether he had a conversation. Then the witness says, "Yes, I recall if I had a conversation. My recollection is that I did not."

Instead ask:

"Did you have a conversation with Mr. Turner?"

"No."

"Do you recall" and "Do you know" are superfluous and sloppy. Just ask the darn question without the preamble. The witness can answer only if she knows. If she doesn't know, make her say so.

"Do you know the time of the collision?"

"Yes."

This really isn't answering what you are asking. You want to know the time of the collision. So ask, "What was the time of the collision?" See, that's not difficult.

For some reason, lawyers have diarrhea of the mouth, and it leads to imprecise questions with ambiguous answers.

"I believe yesterday you testified that Manufacturer B co-operated with the NTSB in doing a comparison of some data on various aircraft. Do you recall that testimony?"

"No."

Now the questioner has to figure out if the "no" means the witness doesn't recall the testimony or that he did not testify as summarized. This leads to confusion and a mangled transcript.

And stop with the "I believe." If you didn't believe it, you wouldn't ask it.

Better is:

"Yesterday, you testified that Manufacturer B cooperated with the NTSB in a comparison of some data on various aircraft, true?" Keep it clear, concise.

Compound questions are always wrong: "What was the time and date of the accident?" That's a lazy question. Sure, you might get a decent answer, but most times the deponent will answer, "About seven p.m." or "December 22nd," and you have to ask again individually anyway.

"What was the date of the accident?"

"May 25, 2007."

"What day of the week was May 25, 2007?"

"Friday."

"At what time did the accident occur on Friday, May 25, 2007?"

And don't be afraid to lead if you know the facts. You can establish a rhythm and bind the witness to the scene.

"On May 25, 2007, you were driving your car?"

"Yes."

"On Main Street?"

"Yes."

"Between Oak and Elm?"

"Yes."

"You were alone in the car?"

"Yes."

"You owned the car?"

"Yes."

"It was daytime?"

"Yes."

"The weather was dry?"

"Yes."

"It wasn't raining, was it?"

"No."

"You were traveling south on Main?"

"Yes."

"Your car was in good working order that day?"

"Yes."

"There was a collision with another vehicle?"

"Yes."

"What time did the collision occur?"

"About a little after one."

"One p.m.?"

"Yeah."

"Tell me what happened."

Of course the more traditional way is to ask, "Did you have an accident on May 25?"

"Yes."

"Were you driving a car at the time of the accident?"

"Yes."

"What was the make and model?"

"On what street?"

"Was anyone else in the car?"

"What was the weather at the time of the accident?"

"In whose car were you driving?"

"In what direction were you traveling?"

It doesn't matter which way you do it, as long as you feel comfortable asking the questions. You can either lead or ask open-ended questions, whichever you prefer. The idea is to bind the witness to a story. The purpose of most depositions is to learn what the witness will testify at the trial. It's also to learn what the witness knows so you can ask others the same questions to determine if there are discrepancies.

If the answers are the usual evasive crap—"I'm not sure who was present. I really don't remember what was discussed"—you can give the witness a taste of cross-examination, but after you obtain all the information he has.

"There was a meeting on February 24, 2006, correct?"

"In the conference room on the 18th floor?"

"The meeting lasted two hours?"

"You were present?"

"For the entire time?"

"And others were present?"

"You testified there were about four other people present?"

"Ms. Burns was one, right?"

"There were another two men and a female, right?"

"Did you introduce yourself to these individuals?"

"Did they introduce themselves to you?"

"But you don't remember their names?"

"So you were at this meeting for two hours with four other people, and you don't remember three of the four names?"

"Did you have a business card?"

"Did you give your card to anyone at the meeting?"

"Did you receive any business cards?"

"Ask for business cards?"

"Was there paper in the room?"

"Were there pens or pencils?"

"Did you write down anyone's name?"

"And you're a vice president of this corporation?"

"Big job?"

"You supervise 23 people?"

"Just so I'm clear, Mr. White, you were in a meeting with four people for two hours and you introduced yourselves all around with pads and pencils and you can't remember their names?"

"You never wrote their names down?"

"Never asked for their business cards?"

And on and on.

You can do this on one aspect of the meeting or on every aspect that the witness has sworn he doesn't remember. I usually do it on only one aspect. Just enough to let the witness and counsel realize how unbelievable the testimony is. Of course, if the witness may not be around for trial, then you may wish to cross-examine as if at trial.

Ask open-ended questions. Sure, cross-examination is fun, but you only question that way if there's no dispute as to facts or after you've obtained the information. Open-ended, non-cross questions are more the rule in a deposition.

"Tell us what you do as vice president of operations."

"Tell us what was discussed at the meeting on January 7."

"Tell us what you did next."

"What did you do after you took Ms. Newman's blood pressure?"

"Then what happened?"

The idea is to get the witness to be a blabbermouth. The more the witness talks, the more you learn.

"So, you were driving on Main on Thursday, December 13, 2007, at about one p.m.—then what happened?"

"Tell us about your job as flight instructor."

"Did you have a procedure where an employee can give notification to management if that employee thought that safety considerations were not being followed?"

"Yes."

"Tell us about this procedure."

Be precise. We live in a world where oral and written communications have many meanings, and witnesses' lawyers will advise them to approach every question as narrowly as they can.

"Did you ever speak to Mr. Gordon about the project?"

"No."

This tells you little. Instead, make the question broader: "Did you ever communicate with Mr. Gordon in any fashion about the project?" Then ask individual questions about e-mail, text messaging, fax, telephone conversations, voice mail, memos, and all the other ways we communicate in this age of technology. And then follow up with:

"Did Mr. Gordon ever speak to you about the project?"

"Did Mr. Gordon ever communicate with you in any fashion about the project?"

Sometimes the questioner will ask a question such as:

"On what date did you attend the staff meeting regarding X?"

"I'm not sure, either January 28 or 29."

Then the questioner will ask a dozen other questions about the meeting and eventually will slip in, "Well, at this staff meeting on January 28, was Ms. Molloy present?"

Your response must be: "Objection, he didn't say the meeting was on the 28th, he testified it was either January 28 or 29." Don't fall asleep.

Pin down what is assumption and what is fact:

"Was Mr. Keller at the meeting on April 8, 2007?"

"I think he was."

"Do you know?"

"No, but he usually goes."

Force the witness to answer the question.

"And you don't know what a Certification Flight Test program is?"

"I don't have precise knowledge of it."

"Well, then, tell us what your knowledge is."

Or: "Have you ever seen a subpoena issued by the Southern District of New York in this case?"

"No."

Follow up. "Have you ever seen a copy of the subpoena . . . ?"

"A subpoena was received by your company, you know that, correct?"

"Yes."

"Do you know who received the subpoena in your company?"

"I believe I already testified that I thought it came into the legal department."

"So you don't know who received it?"

"No, I don't know."

And you can go further: "Did you ever ask who received the subpoena?" "What is the basis of your statement that you thought the subpoena came into the legal department?"

Objections and disputes are designed by experienced defense counsel to disrupt your thinking and your questioning. They want to throw you off balance and off-track. That's why an outline is a necessity. You can battle your adversary and then return to your line of questioning by just glancing at your outline. It's difficult to maintain your composure when you have an adversary who during a dispute will state, "You don't have to raise your voice, Mr. Nolan, please calm down"—knowing that I didn't shout but wanting it to appear in the record that I went berserk. If the deposition is not videotaped, it would appear from that statement that I'm out of control. This tactic can be very effective—sometimes. Remain calm, refute the allegation, then return to questioning. Don't fall for the bait.

These games can't be played if the deposition is videotaped. And you must maintain your demeanor during a videotaped deposition because it records sarcasm or anger as a printed transcript does not.

When you change topics, tell the witness. It can help to introduce a line of questioning: "Now let's discuss the meeting in your office on July 7, 2006." Set the stage with short questions. "You were at the meeting?" "It started about 9:30 a.m. on July 7, 2006?" "It occurred in your office at 250 East 78th Street, New York City, on the 14th floor?" "Now tell us who else was physically present." "Anyone else attend via conference call?" "Any participants by other means?"

Be courteous. This is hard to do in a profession that is littered with conniving fools. You still pick up *The New York Law Journal* and read about a judge sanctioning an attorney for boorish behavior—calling a woman "Hon" or worse. That is unproductive—and bad manners.

It is always better to make a statement on the record and return to questioning than to spend 20 minutes arguing over an objection or documents not produced. The next day, of course, you'll have to back it up by making a motion or contacting the judge so your adversary learns to respect you. Sometimes it's very frustrating because judges don't want to take the time to stop the shenanigans, but my depositions are less contentious than they were years ago, so we are making incremental progress.

Most important, be yourself, not only during depositions but throughout your practice. There's really no right or wrong way. A deposition is for learning facts. Don't forget it.

Settlement Negotiations

Trial lawyers love to fight. Making witnesses squirm, the jury swoon, and the opposition grovel are part of the thrill. Trial lawyers are Clint Eastwoods in Brioni suits. Tough, macho, determined to win. Always ready for trial, always willing to take a verdict.

Yet, the truth is that 97 percent settle. Despite this, no one takes the young associate aside and tells him that his 20-page pretrial brief probably won't be necessary. No one suggests that a lawyer should strive for settlement now or explains how to get there. Litigation often gives lawyers tunnel vision in which the light at the end is a verdict, but verdicts are increasingly rare.

Plaintiffs' lawyers often forget their primary objective is to compensate their clients for injuries. Defense lawyers forget their goal is to minimize their clients' financial losses. For a plaintiff, a $100,000 settlement before filing may be a greater success than a $150,000 verdict three years later. Both sides will most likely save money. The plaintiff may net more, and the defendant will avoid legal fees. The time and aggravation saved is priceless.

Consider the parties' emotions—and the impact of waiting for and then getting a trial result. How will a husband endure years of anger waiting to confront the physician he blames for the loss of his wife? How will the doctor deal with a claim that he caused a patient's death? What if he is found liable and his picture dominates the evening news? How will he explain this to patients, colleagues, his kids?

Often the grinding pressure of litigation persuades parties to settle. Both are then relieved. It doesn't matter that the defendant has been told from the beginning, "Don't worry, the plaintiff doesn't really expect $10 million for a fractured ankle." Don't worry? Your client knows better. He has read the complaint. He has been bombarded with media accounts of million-dollar verdicts for a twisted back. He fears losing his home and business.

Settling soon also eliminates the risk that an unpredictable event will determine the outcome. Between filing the complaint and trial, witnesses disappear or change testimony, injuries heal, and the law changes. Lawyers may be used to unpredictability, but clients can be spared the drama.

Defense counsel usually has an incentive to settle. No longer is it realistic to believe that trial will result in no liability. Juries are mostly sympathetic to plaintiffs. The law—or at least the attitude of most jurors—has evolved to reflect a social policy that places the loss on those who profited from the product or business. Comparative negligence is the norm. Walking away without paying a dime is fabulous, but the cost and stress of trial make every verdict expensive.

One final point in favor of settlement. Some lawyers boast that willingness to settle is weakness. False. In fact, negotiating early may take more guts than proceeding mindlessly with litigation.

Success involves honesty—to yourself, among others. Settling involves an assessment that lawyers may not want to make: confronting weaknesses in your case. In most actions, initial evaluations of experienced lawyers are usually correct. Three years of battle does not change the outcome but merely delays it. Settlement is a success in nearly every dispute.

Here are some helpful rules. Some are basic to trial preparation; others are peculiar to settlement. All are useful.

Investigate early. Not when the case is near trial, but as soon as the phone rings. If you represent the plaintiff, investigate before filing suit. Obtain the hospital records and have an expert decide if malpractice occurred. Take witnesses' statements. If the injury was caused by a product, for example, photograph or video the process. Hire an expert to analyze the product and evaluate its performance.

Talk to the plaintiff and learn her history. It's amazing how many attorneys pigeonhole a case as "a broken leg" or "a concussion" without learning the idiosyncrasies of their client's health history. When discussing settlement, know exactly which vertebrae caused Mr. Campbell to writhe in pain.

Of course, if a prospective client calls, and there's no liability, reject it in writing. Not everyone's injury was caused by someone else's negligence. Recommend two other lawyers for a second opinion. There's nothing worse than taking a case only to learn a year later it's a loser. Then there is nowhere to run or hide.

Defense counsel will also benefit from early investigation. If liability is easily provable, tell your client. If you suspect a crucial witness's testimony is Swiss cheese, full of holes, make sure your client knows. Vetting witnesses and revealing weakness will save time, energy, and, more importantly, money. The plaintiff may welcome a quick resolution, and may accept less than if he had to battle for three years.

Research the law. Open the books to determine whether a legal issue is decisive. Learn the law before you start the action. Know what to emphasize and what to ignore. A lawyer who cites a case or two to refute his adversary's argument in their first discussion will be impressive. The message carries far: If he is this prepared initially, imagine what he will be at trial.

Once you have thorough knowledge of the facts and law, evaluate the case financially. Don't be afraid to call your adversary and suggest mediation. This is not an act of desperation but of pragmatic strength. Provide a reasonable demand if asked. Don't sell your case short, but don't fear entering the process.

Know your venue. Bronx County may border suburban Westchester County, but the counties are worlds apart. In the Bronx, the jurors are angry at hospitals and corporations. They've waited five hours in an emergency room complaining of chest pains only to be told, "Don't worry, it's an upset stomach." That evening the poor mug dies of a heart attack. Plaintiffs' heaven. In Westchester, the juries are conservative suburbanites, and verdicts are low to nonexistent.

Study verdicts and settlements. Talk to the locals who line the courthouse halls. They know the judges, clerks, juries, what works, and what doesn't. Although helpful, this information is only a guide. You know your case best and only you can assess its value.

Learn about your adversary. You will, of course, learn much as the case proceeds. Talk to other lawyers. Is she reasonable? Is everything hardball? If her rep is good—straightforward, no baloney—then ask her how she values the case. Sometimes they tell you. If an insurance carrier is involved, what's its reputation?

Finally, talk to your partners and your spouse and friends. Ask their opinions. Lawyers often speak only to other lawyers. Sometimes it is your bartender who will bluntly reveal that, despite your eloquent recitation of the facts and your intriguing legal defense, your client will lose because what he did "just ain't fair."

Talk to your client. Do this before negotiations commence. Sit down and ask what her expectations are. Inform her how you evaluate the case and explain why. Overvaluing the injuries or minimizing the defendant's exposure may help you be retained but will bite you when discussing settlement.

> "Mrs. Jenkins, great news! The defendant has thrown in the towel and offered $250,000 in settlement."
>
> "Why should I accept that? You promised me $1,000,000."
>
> "When did I say that?"
>
> "Two and a half years ago, when we first met."

Never promise too much. Clients are like elephants; they never forget.

After you discuss the case and legal process, obtain authority to settle. In writing. Do not pressure your client. Let him return home, discuss settlement with family and friends. Make sure they agree with your negotiating strategy. Worst is telling your adversary, "Yeah, that number's fine with me, but my client won't accept it. She changed her mind and now wants . . . ." That ruins future discussions and the other lawyer thinks you're a buffoon.

There are times when reasonable talk about settlement will only anger your client. If emotion rules, then little will be gained by exploring settlement. Likewise, if a defendant is intent on preserving the integrity of his product or his good name, then advise your adversary and prepare for trial. Don't be a showoff and shout, "My client will never settle!" That may make you feel good, but you'll look weak and dishonest if, the day before trial, you e-mail, begging to "have a drink and get rid of this one."

Eventually, I counsel my clients to put aside emotion and decide on settlement or trial based on economics. I can't bring their son back to life. I can't heal the sick or make the blind see. A trial may make them feel better but won't provide what they desperately wish most of all—that the tragedy never occurred. "The only issue is whether you can get more at trial than in settlement," I note diplomatically. But this discussion can only occur well into litigation and at the appropriate time. If done too soon, it will appear callous and will be counterproductive—or it may make the client doubt your commitment. Most clients can appreciate this rationale only after time has lessened their fury.

Many plaintiffs wish to be heard in public—to reveal the goodness of the decedent, the hopes and dreams that were shattered. Usually depositions are emotional for plaintiffs but can be cathartic. After a heartbreaking loss, family members suffer in silence. They avoid discussion of their child or wife for fear that it will cause further sorrow and agony. Unless there's extensive therapy, no spoken outlet exists. No one is told of the horror, the emptiness.

When I perceive this, I often volunteer my client for deposition. Two reasons: to allow a voice that desperately wishes to be heard and to educate my adversary on the goodness of the family, the anguish that will be communicated to a jury. And usually both are achieved.

If you have a recalcitrant defendant who refuses to accept reality, a deposition could provide a taste of the rigors of cross-examination. A thorough and professional deposition often emphasizes what is obvious—insistence on never paying a dime can backfire. Corporate big-shots in their corner offices often need to experience reality. A bruising deposition should tame that outsized ego.

Settlement can be considered any time: before the complaint is filed, before discovery begins, at mediation, at a final pretrial conference, or on the proverbial courthouse steps.

If you are the plaintiff's lawyer, the first time to pick up the phone is before you file suit. Put down your cowboy hat, check your Colt .45 at the door, and call your opposing counsel. Talk and listen.

If they say "We'll never pay a cent," file the complaint. If it's "Sure, let's talk," then talk, but make sure your client's injury has, what I call, "plateaued." You can't negotiate, even if your adversary is amenable, until you're certain that the injury will not become worse. You never want to cash the settlement check and then learn your client needs further surgery. No do-overs in law.

Offer to submit your client for a physical examination. The defendant is entitled to one eventually, and an early examination may help. Wounds heal and the plaintiff will eventually look and feel better. An immediate physical will force the defendant's expert to admit, "Yes, the plaintiff was on crutches when I examined her."

If the defendant's lawyer is missing hospital records or a police report, send them. If you have a witness statement that details negligence, e-mail it. If it helps you, forward it. If not, well, wait until asked.

Don't ever forget the statute of limitations. If it is remotely close, file. You can always negotiate while in discovery.

When the two sides start to exchange numbers, the plaintiff will always demand more than she'll accept and the defendant will offer less. Sometimes you have to play the game. When your adversary is trustworthy, the game can be thankfully brief. With those you don't know, the dance is often a marathon.

I always like to demand as much as possible without having the insurer laugh and hang up the phone. Once dialogue begins, you will know fairly quickly if both parties are serious. A typical mistake by the inexperienced is to demand such an outlandish amount that you never hear the defendant's offer. It's always better to know what the defendant has in mind. You can always say "No thanks."

Another disastrous strategy is to draw a line in the sand: I won't take a penny less than $100,000. So when the offer is $90,000 and the judge wants to split the difference, either you agree (and look foolish and weak) or you try the case (and look stupid and stubborn). Leave yourself some wiggle room. You'll need it.

Be businesslike. Don't slam down the phone when the offer is insulting. Be polite—even with a wiseass. Extract revenge by making him eat his words when he offers you $500,000 after he has said that $150,000 was his top number. When the settlement process is over, you can invite him for a sandwich and politely remind him of his ultimatum.

Skill at negotiating involves some of the same intuition it takes to pick a jury. If the juror smiles at you too much and has all the right answers, you know something is wrong. You should have that same feeling if negotiations are too easy. Review the file to see if you have overlooked something.

Use common sense. And if you don't have any, well then you're on track to be CEO of Fannie Mae. If you're unsure of whether to accept an offer, then wait. Give yourself time. Talk to your partners, your client. Then decide.

Before rejecting any offer, discuss it with your client. Malpractice looms when you reject an offer your clients would accept, only to learn that the offer has been withdrawn. Now the case has to be tried, and you better win.

Don't apologize for weakness your opponent recognizes. Confront it without alarm. Explain that you will counter with expert testimony, with a unique legal theory, with a motion in limine that may eliminate it. Or admit it, and advise that you considered it in your demand.

Don't offer or demand a range of two figures at the same time. "We'll settle this case for $40,000 to $50,000" means that you have just demanded $40,000 to settle. Do not be equivocal: "I am authorized to offer $75,000, and that's almost it." Why should the plaintiff settle for less than "it?" "We'll pay $60,000, but that's getting close to my authority." The plaintiff's lawyer is not your pal; he wants to squeeze the last dollar out of you. Why should he accept this offer when you have signaled you will pay more?

Don't bid against yourself. Every time a demand is lowered, an offer must be raised. If your demand is within reason, you should have an offer in response. You can dance around the verbal boxing ring bobbing and weaving to determine if there's another offer. But if none emerges, end this round of negotiations.

Decide where you will make your stand and do not deviate from it. Your client must understand each move. With your client's approval, you can try the case over a difference of $5,000. Whether you convey your bottom line before bringing suit or at the eve of the trial, you must mean it.

To these general rules I add some cautions:

- First, maintain records of settlement discussions. Negotiations heat up and cool down; lawyers, adjusters change; recollections fail. Written records help.
- Second, a warning about a person who may become a mediator: the judge. A judge can be crucial in bringing your unreasonable opponent to the bargaining table. But approach this three-way negotiation with caution, for the judge may want to drive a harder bargain than you are prepared to make. Even a judge can learn that once you've given an ultimatum, you intend to keep it.
- Once the trial starts, settlement negotiations need not end. They may continue until the verdict is read and even through the appeal. Of course, you should be prepared to try your case. But also be prepared to settle. Sometimes you will be happily surprised.

Jury Selection

The room is cramped, barren, uninviting. There are no windows and only one door. The floor is dirty, the chairs uncomfortable. The walls are painted, as we say in Brooklyn, puke green. No, this is not an Afghan torture chamber; it is jury selection in state court in New York City.

You, the great trial lawyer, will spend the next day or week with your adversaries, trying to influence jurors into favoring your client before they hear a word of testimony. Wait, did I say that? What I mean, of course, is trying to select fair and impartial jurors.

Jury selection is a battle for the hearts and minds of triers of fact—six or 12 ordinary citizens living ordinary lives and bothering no one, until they received a hated jury summons in the mail. Now they must travel to court, try to get excused, and, failing that, wait around all day listening to lawyers talk sanctimoniously (and hypocritically) about fairness, justice, and the American Way. Maybe waterboarding is preferable.

But remember: Jurors decide whether you win or lose. Be careful and do it right. Remember, if you don't, you can fail, and in our business, that means losing. By examining jurors' reactions to you and what you say, you may determine that the juror who swears he can give your disabled client a fair shake is really thinking that he has had it with those million-dollar verdicts and is going to fix this system—right now! Or you uncover that the juror who promises to

69

be fair to General Motors secretly has had it in for GM ever since his Chevy conked out on the way to Lover's Lane in 1986.

So, in those jurisdictions that still allow the art form that is jury selection, remember a few guidelines.

Know the rules. Federal court is not state court—and vice versa. (Heck, increasing numbers of federal courts don't allow real voir dire at all.) Each courthouse and judge is different. No one, it seems, has the same procedures. If you simply assume that you know the rules, you could be wrong. Do you have to submit voir dire questions? Are you allowed to question potential jurors? When do you request peremptory challenges? How many do you have? In a multidefendant case, one judge allowed only a total of three peremptory challenges because the attorneys failed to request additional challenges when they submitted voir dire questions.

What system for challenges is in effect? Some courts hold that if you don't excuse Juror No. 1, and instead excuse Juror No. 2, then Juror No. 1 is sworn. If you don't excuse them, they're in. Other courts will not swear any juror until all are sworn so that a juror can be excused at any time. To learn the ground rules, talk to colleagues and court personnel.

Know your jury pool. If you're trying a case in an unfamiliar jurisdiction, arrive a few days early. Walk around town. Get a haircut. Grab a burger at Joe's Diner. Have a beer in a neighborhood saloon. Forget about the four-star restaurants; those people won't be on the jury. Talk to people in the street. Read the local papers. Get a feel for the community and its people.

Look at how people react. If they hide their pocketbooks when they say, "You must be from New York," then hire local counsel to sit with you at trial. If you're from New York City, but the trial isn't there, make sure you tell the jury (and the judge) that it wasn't your fault where you were born. Apologize—tell them you're a Brooklyn kid. Otherwise, you may be seen as a liberal phony with a loud mouth and an outsized ego. If you can afford extensive jury surveys, then use them. But talk to and observe ordinary citizens for a few days before you begin. What works in New York or Los Angeles might not work in Knoxville or Santa Fe.

Speak to the jury. If your jurisdiction allows you to question the jurors, do so. Do not waive that right. If you're in federal court, ask the judge to allow you to pose voir dire questions. Most often this is denied. But ask anyway. On occasion, you may be allowed to address the jury. If the judge insists on seeing voir dire questions before selection, submit them in detail. In federal court, request that the judge ask questions you submitted. Many times federal judges ignore voir dire requests, and you must explain why they are crucial. If you represent Citigroup, tell the judge it is important to learn if any juror believes all bankers are crooks.

If you are finally allowed to address the jury panel, use the opportunity effectively. Explain what you are doing and obtain information on job, family, education, jury service, experience with lawsuits, and knowledge of the parties and their lawyers. Even though you risk being boring and repetitious, do not be intimidated into being cursory or flippant.

Look at the jury. What are they wearing? Air Jordans or business shoes? Suits or work shirts? Do they have dirt under their fingernails? What are they reading—*People* or *The New York Times*? Are their clothes worn or new? What is their reaction to the lawyers—one of openness or the usual distrust and disgust? Do they talk to their neighbors or sit alone refusing to remove their coats? Take note of their age, sex, race, ethnic group. Are they wearing religious medals, political emblems, or social buttons? Usually it makes no difference, for most jurors try hard to be fair and impartial. But we are all weak; we are all biased to some degree. Your job is to limit the chance that a juror with a preconceived bias will be selected.

Does a prospective juror appear hostile? This shows obvious contempt not only for you but for the system. If someone is bored after two hours and you are facing a six-week trial, think twice about allowing that person to sit, especially if you have a complex defense that requires mental acuity or stamina. Sometimes, the opposite problem comes up: The prospective juror looks too eager. He is the one who may have his mind made up. He is the one who is going to fix this system that is too expensive and too slow, and that gives away money like politicians' promises.

Be considerate. Most court facilities, even if in decent repair, are inadequate. My theory is that there's a direct correlation between the adequacy of court facilities and the verdict. As courthouses deteriorate, plaintiffs' verdicts increase, In federal court, with clean rooms and stenographers on time, awards are substantially less than in the dilapidated Bronx and Brooklyn courthouses where the roofs leak, bathrooms stink, and "Mark loves Diane" is carved into the courtroom benches. The newer the courthouse, the more defense verdicts. In fact, if insurance companies really want to save money, they should funnel their funds into sprucing up the courthouses so that the jurors' anger would not be visited on them.

When you address the jurors, speak as equals. Too many lawyers begin by explaining what voir dire means this way: "It is a French term meaning . . . ." What the attorney is really saying is "I am educated and understand French and you don't." In the back, a truck driver is thinking that he hasn't cared about French since he flunked it in high school, but he sure doesn't like that idiot in the gray suit whose case doesn't sound so hot anyway.

Take a break for coffee in the morning. Ask the judge if the panel can have an extra 15 minutes for lunch. Understand if they are delayed on the train or freeway; they are not necessarily lazy. Be an example; appear on time. Be prepared and organized. If the jurors see that you believe this case is important, they will treat it the same way.

Realize that jurors don't want to be there. They would prefer to be at their jobs or with their families. For some, it is an extreme sacrifice; they have small businesses or jobs that they cannot leave for two or three weeks at a clip. Remember, you are being very well paid to talk to them; they are not being well paid (to put it mildly) to listen to you. Treat them as human beings. "Is it Miss, Mrs., or Ms.?" Don't ask, "Do you have a job or are you a housewife?" Don't make fun of their jobs. "Oh, so you're the guy I can blame when my train breaks down. . . ." Treat them as you would want to be treated.

Speak English. Leave the legalese for the cocktail parties where you can impress your cousins from New Jersey, Forget "prior to" and "subsequent to." Don't ask "What was the highest level of education you achieved?" Ask "How far did you get in school?" Don't ask "What is your occupation?" Ask "Tell me about what you do for a living" or "Where do you work?"

Ask open-ended questions. The idea is not for you to talk and talk and talk, but rather to listen to jurors—the more they reveal, the better. Ask short questions that will have them talking a lot. "Tell me about your family." "Tell me about your education." "Tell me about your experiences with doctors and hospitals." "Have you ever been in a car accident? Tell me about it." Have them talk in paragraphs, not in simple "yes" or "no" answers.

If your case is a media sensation, ask "What have you heard about my client?" Sure, you will get answers that you won't like, but at least you can confront them before the trial starts. For every potential juror who blurts out something bad, there are at least two others who are thinking the same. You may not be able to eradicate all knowledge, but you can address it, try to minimize it, and have the jurors promise not to let preconceptions cloud their judgment. Then, at closing, remind them of their pledge.

Admit weaknesses. If you represent a driver whose blood alcohol level was higher than A-Rod's batting average, tell the jury. The test results won't go away. Ask if they can be fair even though your client had a few. "Ladies and gentlemen, you are going to hear sooner or later that my client had been drinking. Can you wait until you hear all the evidence before you make up your mind? If you can't give a person who has been drinking a fair shake, that's okay, as long as you admit it now. If you become a juror and you judge him simply on the fact that he was drinking, and you reach a final conclusion without waiting to hear all the testimony, then you really wouldn't be doing your job as a juror." Ask each individual juror. Some will say it depends on how much he was drinking. You can work on them so that they excuse themselves by admitting they could not be fair. Some will not admit their bias, but you and the other jurors will see through this charade; and when you use a peremptory, all jurors will understand.

Many jurors are angry at banks, Wall Street, and the government. If you're defending a criminal white-collar case, you must confront this emotion and try to neutralize it. Politicians and talking heads call for indictments and jail time for those perceived responsible for our economic problems. Acknowledge this reality in your jury questionnaires and through your questions to potential jurors. Force jurors either to admit this bias (and excuse them for cause) or to promise that they will not allow this anger to influence their determination of guilt.

If you are defending a drug company or a hospital whose negligence has resulted in a severely brain-damaged infant who cannot walk, talk, or care for herself, make sure you condition the jury before they see the child in court. Tell them there is no question about the seriousness of the infant's injuries; that they will see Jennie and that she will not be able to walk or talk; that we feel very sympathetic, but we did not cause her condition. Go into detail; explain all her problems—how she must be fed, how she is thin and small. Prepare the jury for the impact. Do not allow them to walk into the courtroom thinking that they will hear a simple medical malpractice or product liability case, only to be shocked by seeing a helpless, beautiful, wheelchair-bound infant.

All people have some sympathy. If you represent the defendant, advise the jurors that it is normal to feel sad when they hear of the plaintiff's injuries. But they must not let that interfere with their judgment—they must be strong and rule in favor of the defendant if that is what the evidence proves. Condition potential jurors to make a tough decision so they are able to look at little Jennie and her mother and still rule for the defendant.

Tell the jurors they have alternatives. If a juror is wavering and is unsure whether she can be fair, explain that there are other cases in the courthouse—criminal, medical malpractice, breach of contract, real estate. She "may feel more comfortable sitting on a different type of jury." If a juror informs you that her mother was killed in a car accident, that same juror may insist she can be fair to the defendant. Hogwash. Kick her off the jury. Have her admit underlying resentment. Have the juror come to the realization by asking the following questions:

"Now, Mrs. Smith, you tell us that your mother, unfortunately, was in an automobile accident. Well, I represent the person who must defend this lawsuit. It involves a similar accident. I have to go back to him and say that all these jurors promise to be fair and impartial. Now, could you look my client in the eye and tell him that you can be fair and impartial even though this trial may bring back unpleasant memories of your mother's death?" Usually, the answer remains "Yes." Continue: "Isn't it possible you might bend over just a little to assist the plaintiff subconsciously?" Try to have the juror excuse herself. But don't push. If there's resistance, do not overdo the questions. Use a peremptory challenge. That's what they're for.

Don't confront or embarrass a juror. A juror may be unemployed. Don't ask, "How long have you been out of work?" Don't ask if he's prejudiced. Tell the juror that you represent an Arab corporation—is there any problem with giving a Saudi Arabian company a fair shake? If a juror's face stiffens and through clenched teeth he says he can be fair, don't ask "Are you prejudiced against Arabs?" His answer will be "No." The bigot—and all jurors—will resent the question, because no one believes he is prejudiced. Everyone is always fair. To contend that someone cannot be fair is to state that someone cannot be American and does not believe in democracy. Look at facial expressions, body language. Ask jurors their opinion of the corporation or of Saudi Arabia. You might obtain a damaging statement that allows you to challenge for cause.

Trust your instincts. If you represent a Hispanic plaintiff, you may want other Hispanics on the jury. Yet that doesn't often work. If your jury survey tells you that a young, married woman is perfect, but there is something you don't like about this particular young, married woman, kick her off.

You can often identify whether a juror will be good or bad simply by demeanor. Some are so angry that it is obvious—even when they provide answers they think you want to hear. Jurors are like most people: They tell you what you want to hear. "How are you today?" is always answered with "Fine" even though the speaker may have had the most miserable morning.

Almost never use your last peremptory. Inevitably, the juror who replaces the one excused is always worse.

Jury selection is not a trial. Occasionally, a lawyer is so satisfied with jury selection that he believes he has won. Wrong. The case must still be tried. Jury selection doesn't mean anything if your client, case, or proof is deficient. Voir dire is only one aspect of the trial. It's important, but not as much as the evidence or the testimony. You can't rest once jury selection is completed. Your job has just begun.

Opening Statement

A skeptical jury awaits. Citizens, bored and a touch angry, sit silently as the judge drones on. They glance around the dreary courtroom, at the sallow walls, the cynical clerk, the few spectators. They want to connect the bits and pieces heard in jury selection. They want action and suspense, like in the movies.

Then the judge peers over her glasses, mumbles your name and other words you don't hear as your mind races and your hands tremble. You jerk your head from your notes, breathe deeply, and suddenly you're focused. You stand, thank the court, nod at your adversaries, stride to the podium, adjust your notes, and pause. All eyes focus on you and, with a slight smile, you look those calloused jurors in the eye, and with a clear, crisp voice, you begin.

It's time to tell your story—to be thorough and logical, to detail the facts, touch on the law, persuade the jury that you should and will win. After all, people say studies show juries decide immediately after opening, so, if you flub it, confuse, hesitate, or are not convincing, you'll lose them and probably the case.

The opening is what you've been anticipating. It's an opportunity to teach, to explain, to introduce your client and case, to describe the suffering, to appeal to the jury's intelligence, sense of fairness, and to tug, just a little, on their emotions. It's a chance to argue in such a reasoned, compelling manner that the case is over before the dopey defendants' attorneys utter a word.

It sounds easy, simple perhaps. After all, you were the star on the debate team in high school, and last week at O'Sullivan's Pub, everyone roared as you told joke after joke. But this is for real. It's what you get paid for. Not to come in second or just to do a good job, but to win. This isn't kids' soccer or basketball where everyone plays and they don't keep score.

There's no more "It's how you played the game" crap. You lose and your partners, client, spouse are livid. You spent how long and how much money? And you got zilch? Or the jury awarded that sleazy plaintiff more than it cost to build an aircraft carrier. How come you didn't settle? Are we going to lose the client and its billings? What the eff happened, as my angelic daughter would put it.

I don't know when jurors decide. I'm not certain if the opening is the whole game. It's probably a roller coaster—one day they favor the plaintiff, the next the defendant. But I do know this: You may not win the case on opening, but you sure as heck don't want to lose it then. It's hard to run uphill, to realize your adversary connected with the jury, was thorough, knowledgeable, and convincing—and you were not. Sure the case is obvious, the facts simple, the law rudimentary. It's a grubby appeal to their emotions: Surely they can't throw out the widow or the maimed iron worker without a sou. It's a slam dunk, right? Let the defendant try to explain away the negligence, the death, the tragedy. No way. Then your opening is sloppy, confusing, while your adversary is clear and convincing. Your smirk freezes, you nervously reach for water, and quietly curse your silly arrogance and foolish laziness. Get your butt in gear or you'll be having nightmares for a decade if this easy one goes down the tubes.

Prepare thoroughly. This is obvious. You absolutely must prepare—thoroughly and frequently. Have a written outline detailing all the points you wish to emphasize. If you plan to cite a specific regulation, document, or e-mail, write it word for word and don't be afraid to read it so you don't screw up. Incorporate language from the probable jury charge in your argument, but have it in writing so you can use the exact language.

Sure I'd like to open without notes and be as charming as Ronald Reagan or inspire like Bill Clinton, but I'm me, on occasion eloquent but mostly mediocre. I often can't remember what I had for breakfast, so I drag my notes with me, like a legal security blanket. Juries are interested in information not flair. This isn't Olympic figure skating where you win points for style. Get the job done. Don't forget anything. Winning ugly is better than losing beautiful.

But don't write every word and read it unless you're hopelessly inept. Have some spontaneity. If you simply stand at the podium and read in a monotone, you'll lose the jury and your message.

Practice, practice, practice. Hire the mock jury guys and have them critique your work. Videotape your performance. You'll be surprised at what you learn. The opening is the one part of the trial where you can know pretty much exactly what you'll say, especially if you're the plaintiff. Even defendants will know 95 percent of what they'll say. If you can't afford jury consultants, practice in front of the mirror, to your assistant, partners, associates, anyone. Listen to criticism but not to the patronizing gray-hair who wants to change every word, because back in 1978 he had a trial and did it this way. It's your case. Think Sinatra: Do it your way.

When you practice, make sure the listener is able to follow your argument. Periodically stop and ask him to summarize what was just said. A polished opening that no one understands is worthless. Years ago, a famous trial practice guru actually tried a case—an important, high-profile case—and kept using the phrase *red herring* in his opening. Only one problem: No juror knew what that meant. There were later reports that, in the jury room, some on the panel tried to figure out where the evidence was about the fish. What is obvious to you is not so to the ordinary stiff, who brown-bags to work every day. Jurors know phonies, and speaking over their heads sends off phony signals. Everyone hates phonies. Ask Holden Caulfield.

Use simple language. We watch the Super Bowl and "American Idol," "Jersey Shore," and "Dancing with the Stars"; we read tabloids and *People,* obsess over Angelina and Brad. For most jurors, that goes double, so drop the Shakespearean references, the vocabulary words learned while cramming for the SATs.

You're dealing with honest, good, proud people who hate—just despise—haughty, condescending types who know more and just have to flaunt it. You have more formal education, but that doesn't mean you're smarter. I never saw a course in street smarts on any college or law school curriculum. And those Masters of the Universe with their MBAs from Wharton and Columbia turned out to be pretty dumb as they ran our financial institutions into oblivion.

Speak to jurors the same way you wish to be addressed. Before Brooklyn became hip (alas), I could tell that those Manhattan or suburban denizens really didn't mean "That's nice," when I told them where I live. Their demeanor and tone shouted, "Why would anyone live in Brooklyn with the gum-chewing bridge-and-tunnel crowd?" And I'm sure you've had the same experience, whether from a pompous senior partner, a sneering classmate, or someone you met at a cocktail reception. The kind of person who holds the wineglass by the stem, asks where you summer, or (my favorite) who peers over your head to find someone important as they shake your hand. If you're like that in your opening, you can, as we say in Brooklyn, "Fuhgeddaboutit."

Educate the jury. Whether you have a simple auto case or a complicated product liability matter, you must educate the jury. Explain the product, the behavior, and the documents so they can visualize what occurred. This isn't easy when dealing with complex business contracts, the design of a truck, or technical language concerning medical issues, securities matters, or complex credit-default swaps. No matter how complex the matter, you have to simplify so the jury can get it. Take your time and detail the facts and subject thoroughly. Make sure the jury is educated from your lips rather than your adversary's.

Argue and ask. The plaintiff has to tell the jury what he will prove. "The evidence will prove . . . ." And what he wants. "At the end of this trial, I want you to give a verdict for Mrs. Clark and award her money damages . . . ." Don't be shy. If you want a boatload of dough, tell them. You don't have to use numbers, but make sure they understand you will be asking for more than they'll ever make in five lifetimes.

As a defendant, if you want the jury to toss the pathetic plaintiff and his wheelchair into the middle of Court Street, tell them. If the plaintiff was fired because he was a lazy, incompetent bum and not because of his race, religion, or sex, shout it. If you don't, they may never know. Don't be subtle. And don't wait until closing. It may be too late.

If your theme is that the defendant was told a million times that the product was dangerous, repeat it during opening. If you have evidence that plaintiff's a malingerer, sing that chorus constantly. Stare at the jurors when you state that you will prove your case, sustain your burden, making sure they understand it's not "beyond a reasonable doubt," which is all they've ever heard. Do it without theatrics, professionally and convincingly but without hyperbole.

The defendant should appeal to the jurors' courage, fairness, and common sense in peeking around and through the horrible injuries. "American justice demands you award plaintiff nothing." "Enter judgment for my client, Exxon, because even large corporations that make billions and employ thousands deserve the same fair shake as you and me and all Americans." In short, opening is not a place to be coy. If it's important, mention it. If you want something, say exactly what it is.

Judges usually limit emotional displays—"Save it for closing, Counselor"—so you may have to seek a middle ground between swinging from the chandeliers and a boring soliloquy that has the jury snoring after 15 minutes.

Use demonstrative evidence. PowerPoint, videos, photos: Show the crucial evidence to the jury so your words are supported by signed letters, handwritten notes, e-mails. Use a media consultant if your technical knowledge is so low that you don't know how to post a photo on your Facebook page. Young lawyers know this stuff, so have them prepare an inexpensive, effective computer presentation. Words are powerful, but pictures and videos can seal the deal.

Keep your word. There's nothing worse than vowing to prove this and that, and then having nothing. Note your adversary's promises. If she doesn't deliver, tap dance all over her lack of credibility at closing. In an auto case, defense counsel promised to prove three things, including bringing an expert to testify that my client's injuries were bogus. He failed on all three. The first words in my closing: Remember last week during openings when Mr. Jones stood in front of this jury, before this honorable court, and vowed to prove X, Y, and Z. I waited and waited and then he rested. He said his proof was complete and never proved X or Y or Z. Nada, zilch. Oh, you can have fun with that one.

If you're unsure of your strategy, leave some wiggle room. Don't brag about what you'll do if you're uncertain whether it will occur.

Openings provide the jury with information and comprehension. You can orate, persuade, and be eloquent and brilliant in hopes of laying the groundwork for success. Opening is important, but remember this, too: It's really a tiny skirmish in a much larger battle. Once opening is completed, you move to the grind of trial, with witnesses and exhibits and unexpected answers and constant headaches. Testimony and evidence win trials, yet an effective opening provides clarity and rationale for why you should win. Don't blow it.

Direct Examination

Direct testimony: It's boring and as sexy as varicose veins. As the examining lawyer, you stand before the jury in your navy blue suit, the same as you wore to your first Communion, hair neatly combed, looking and sounding like Al Gore on a slow day. In your mind, you can still hear your mother telling you to stand up straight and your old third-grade teacher, Mrs. Lynch, imploring you to enunciate and leave your Brooklyn accent in the schoolyard. Soon the big moment arrives, and you ask the crucial question, the never-to-be-forgotten "And then what happened?"

Despite its pedestrian reputation, direct examination is crucial, and deserves better. Direct is the opening act, not for you as the great trial lawyer, but for the person who actually wins or loses the case—your client. It is the client whom the jury scrutinizes, whom the jury likes or despises, whom the jury believes. Of course, you have been taught that jury selection and the opening statement determine victory. The message seems to be that a persuasive trial lawyer is more a magician than Merlin. But it is your clients—and not you—who win and lose the everyday cases, through their dress, their looks, and, especially, their direct testimony.

Other kinds of testimony have more inflated reputations, of course: Everyone can produce experts whose credentials are so impressive (sounding) that a jury cannot distinguish someone who is real from

83

someone who could not find a subway in New York City. You put on seven experts, the defense has eight. Yours were educated at Harvard, hers at Yale. An expert standoff is almost a certainty.

Cross-examination—the golden child of trial practice teachers—is for Armani ties, for laughter and indignation, for running about the courtroom with menacing stares and boisterous objections. It can be used to bludgeon a witness into submission or cause a thousand paper cuts that are precise, clean, and eventually fatal. Cross-examination pervades, even over-occupies, our thoughts during trial. We keep that notepad on our night table so we can write the killing questions when we awaken from our Perry Mason dreams of victory. We practice cross in our bathrooms, we brag about it at conferences and cocktail parties. We know it because we like it. We are good at it because we study it.

But cross is not as important as its image. After stripping away the CLE veneer, you see the client. It is she who makes the case. And the first peek at the client is on direct examination. If the jury doesn't accept that testimony, the case is lost. Cross-examination won't matter. So, though it may not excite lawyers, direct examination is often most important in a lawsuit. Here are a few guidelines.

Know your witness. If you first meet your witness the day before trial, it's too late. There will be no rapport, no confidence. By trial, there are a score of disasters to deal with. Your expert has had the audacity to drop dead. Your fact witness has fled the snow and smog of New Jersey for a cozy condo near Disney World. With trial looming, you won't have the time to concentrate on the client's emotional needs. Will he cry, become angry, fall apart? Will he ever shut up? Does he tell you his family history if you ask if he is married? Is he intelligent? Nervous? Street-smart? Shy? Are his children tattooed, with rings in their noses? Is he fat, bald, and ugly? Does he speak English well enough to dispense with an interpreter? (A sure way to peeve the judge and jury is to have a client admit he does not speak English that well at the start of a trial and have no interpreter in sight.)

Learn these things beforehand—long, long beforehand. Otherwise, you are lost.

Appearances count. If you want money from a jury, forget the Rolex, gold chains, and *My Cousin Vinny* look. Don't force a tie and jacket on a truck driver. When in doubt, dress conservatively. Teenagers are trouble, but most juries will understand their craziness. If you're in small-town Indiana, forget the tasseled shoes and double-breasted suits. If your client is in court for weeks, a different outfit each day is revealing.

Know your file. Spend the time. Review facts and testimony, question by question. Do not assume that your sophisticated, cultured executive witness will come across well. The relationship is fairly constant: the more educated, the better paid, then the more arrogant and condescending. Wipe that Manhattan "I know what's best for you" smirk from his face. Your jury will be ordinary folks whose thrill is the Super Bowl or a good hamburger, not those who believe heaven is a 2001 Bordeaux or *The New Yorker*'s "Talk of the Town" column. If the jury believes that your defendant-witness is a devotee of the "Only the little people pay taxes" school, you can add another zero to the plaintiff's verdict.

Make sure the witness knows what is critical, what will wound him, and—above all—how to give a straightforward answer.

> *Q:* Is this photograph a fair and accurate representation of Westholme Avenue on the date you moved to your new office?
>
> *A:* Well, I'm not really sure what you mean by that.

Even the judge may stop working his crossword puzzle when he hears that. The jury will suspect that there may be something amiss with the photograph even after it is admitted into evidence. A witness on direct must know exactly what he is supposed to know.

Use a video camera when you practice testimony. It can be invaluable. It lets the witness see himself—and you see yourself. Listen to how you and the witness sound. You don't need professional audiovisual experts, just a tripod or someone to hold the camera. Half an hour is sufficient. Your ego (and the witness's) will not accept your errors (and his) until you see and hear them.

Rehearse in front of real people. If you have doubts about how you or your witness comes across, ask someone who will know and will tell you the truth. Forget about a young associate. She will tell you what you want to hear; anyway, attending law school has seriously compromised her powers of perception. Forget your secretary or paralegal. He has enough work already. Get someone off the street, a friend, a husband.

Years ago, my partners tried the Pan Am/Lockerbie case. Much of the testimony was reading depositions. I was asked to play the part of a particularly important and favorable witness during one such read-through. I thumbed through the testimony the night before to see if there were any names I could not pronounce. On the stand, I read the testimony in a serious voice—after all, it was serious testimony. I thought I was Laurence Olivier.

When I finished, one of our clients asked me if the testimony I had read was supposed to help us. She said my voice and demeanor were so "stern" she wasn't sure. I'm afraid the jury was equally confused. I failed to realize that the manner of my testimony was almost as important as the content. The cure is simple: Next time, buy your plumber a pizza and set him in front of the VCR to review the videotape of the direct. See if it works.

Welcome your experts to the real world. During a medical-malpractice action, the defendant doctor's expert provided testimony so convoluted, so snarled with medical terms, that my cross could be very brief because I was sure that the jury did not understand a word he said. In fact, I couldn't follow him, either. Forget the mumbojumbo. Speak real English. Remember that the expert must be a teacher. Unfortunately, most professors—and the groves of academe are this nation's principal expert breeding ground—are terrible teachers. They are boring and aloof and adhere to the philosophy that "you must understand me. I do not have to make myself understood."

On the witness stand, this is death. The expert must explain the meanings of all technical terms. Interrupt him and ask: "You have used the term *discount rate*. Please tell us what you mean by discount rate." Have him use examples, analogies, anything that will help the jury learn your case. Use charts, blackboards, blow-ups, videos, not only to keep the jury awake, but to teach. The expert must speak the jury's language. It is up to you to make sure she does.

Know your courtroom and the judge. Go to the courthouse. Find out if you are in an antique building with majestic ceilings and parking lot dimensions. Be especially alert for courts with sound systems from the megaphone era. Is there anything more annoying than the constantly repeated phrase, "Please keep your voice up so the entire jury can hear you"? If you are in such a building, then teach your client to be loud. A good witness who cannot be heard is almost the same as no witness at all.

Have the witness look at the jury. Right in the eye. Most witnesses look only at the lawyer. Tell the witness to look at the jury from time to time. This is especially important for experts. You need to scope out the layout of the court to determine how difficult eye contact will be.

Have the witnesses available. If the judge moves the case like he gets paid for results, then you better have the witness in the hallway. "Judge, my witness will be here in an hour" just won't cut it in some courtrooms. If your witness isn't available, some judges will immediately announce that the plaintiff or defendant rests. Your malpractice insurer may have to be notified or, worse, you may have to explain to your partners why your long-standing corporate client ($3 million in yearly billings) is sending work to another firm.

Use notes. Lawyers fall into two groups: those who write down everything and those who disdain paper. The latter think, "I'm the greatest, I don't need help." That is the cry of those who are convinced they know everything, but know little. Write out the important questions: the hypotheticals, the expert opinion questions, the foundation questions for the admission of evidence, the exact words to introduce documents into evidence. Do not let your ego—or decades of trial practice seminars—prevent you from sometimes reading a question or looking at notes. Even on direct, your mind is racing—you're trying to listen, you want to determine if your client is effective, you need to anticipate cross-examination or an objection—plus, everyone is looking at you. Panic is not far away. Even if you never use it, just knowing that you have the questions on paper is calming.

Think of Barack's taking the oath of office from Chief Justice Roberts. Two Harvard Law grads stepping on the other's lines and then Roberts mixing up the words because he was so smart he didn't need to have it written. So they screwed it up and had to redo it the next day.

Be organized. Have your exhibits at your fingertips. Have copies for the judge and the jury to save time. If your case involves a ton of documents, buy binders for the jurors so that they can insert each document as it is admitted into evidence. Don't flail around the courtroom trying to locate a document. Testimony is like music; it should have a rhythm, a beat. Interruptions to have six or eight jurors read a document take time. The mood will change. Your adversary, who watched with growing horror as your client was effective, and as the testimony gained momentum, will be ecstatic as a document is laboriously passed from one juror to another.

Let the witness perform. It's not your show. You should try to fade into the background. Put the spotlight on the witness chair. Ask questions that lead to narrative: "Tell us about your family." "Tell us about what happened on July 13, 2010." "What happened at that meeting?" Unless the witness has real problems saying anything well, let him talk. Let the jury know the witness through background questions about his family, education, and work. Start slowly, easing the client into the rhythm of the trial. All witnesses are nervous. Build confidence by throwing softballs. Do not lead; allow the testimony to be in paragraphs, not sentences or single words. If the jury seems to be having trouble following, interrupt for a clarification. Otherwise, shut up. It's her game to win or lose.

Listen to the answer. It's not easy. A million thoughts are fighting for attention during direct: Your expert just told you that he cannot be available Friday morning but will be all set for Monday. Now you have to stall, which is not your style, or ask the judge to put the case over until Monday. The hospital records that were subpoenaed have arrived—but they are on a CD.

If, despite all these distractions, you fail to listen, and if you just follow your script, you may miss an important point. No matter how many times you rehearse, at least one surprise always pops out of the witness stand.

> *Q:* What color was the light as you approached the intersection?
> *A:* It was red.
> Red flags, sirens, those car alarms that wake you at three a.m. should be pounding your brain. [Green, you idiot, we went over this a million times.] Damage control:

Q: Well, I'm talking about as you approached the intersection about a block away, [Mr. Moron].

A: Well, it was first red and then turned to green.

Q: When you were two blocks away the light was red, right?

Objection, leading.

Sustained.

Q: Between the site of the collision and Main Street, which is one block, the light was green, correct?

Objection, Judge, he's testifying again.

If my client's testifying is upsetting Ms. Hall, I'll rephrase.

By now, your witness should have gotten the hint. Listen to the answers. They will surprise you.

Use demonstrative evidence. Talk is enhanced by visuals. How long can anyone listen to All-Talk Radio without turning it off? Maybe 30 or 45 minutes, but never an hour. Yet we ask the jury to listen to testimony, much of it bland, for hours at a stretch. By its nature, direct is dull. Liven it up. Use photos, enlarge records, use charts. Consider videos, computer-enhanced graphics, and other high-tech equipment with visual appeal.

Move the witness toward the jury. Get her off the stand and let her use the charts. Let the jury see the witness, especially an expert, and not just the head and shoulders. Have the expert doctor stand before the jury when he demonstrates the injury with a model or an X-ray. Make the courtroom like Oprah, relaxed and interactive. Don't chain yourself to the podium, and free the witness from the witness chair.

The value and effect of direct examination is often minimized, since it's straightforward without the glitter and glamour of other aspects of the trial. Yet, it is when the jury first hears from your witness and often will decide not only the credibility of the testimony but the merits of your case.

Cross-Examination

The idea is to destroy—credibility, confidence, demeanor. Rapid-fire pointed questions designed to rattle. "Yes or No," you order in a stern, loud bark. The witness squirms, hesitates, searches for escape. You pounce, "Yes or no, Sir?" With a sigh, he responds meekly, his spirit broken, his will exhausted. You have him. Your approach softens a little, and you go a bit slower, but still with a firm sarcastic tone. The jury's awake, heads nodding. You pick up the pace. He doesn't resist. He's yours. You'll dream about this moment for months, years, maybe always.

This is the payoff for all the tedious work, the years of exasperating depositions, the hours listening to the pompous instruct on proper techniques at trial practice seminars, the miserable mandatory mediations, the anguish of so many last-second settlements. Finally, you're a real lawyer. You've arrived.

After all, law should be fun. Well, at least a little. It can be satisfying at times, even enjoyable when a thank-you box of chocolates arrives. Exposing exaggerations, lies, forcing a witness to admit you're right—a good, crisp, devastating cross is a hoot. Now you can join the war-story old-timers in the courthouse halls pontificating about the time when . . . .

Of course, a knockout cross is as rare as a kind word from one of your teenagers. Partly, this is because the number of trials has decreased. At a recent bar event, a colleague mentioned that, back in the day, they'd always have at least six partners on trial defending med-mal cases. Now, there are maybe one or two. The reason mentioned by clients, judges, court administrators, and insurers is universal—*trials are just too damn expensive.*

Fortunately, they're not extinct. Trials occur, although not like when I first was admitted. Then, at calendar call, judges would screech at the defense attorney, "You got money?" Any hesitation would result in a no-nonsense "Select." Everyone picked a jury, including the timid law student who appeared in Bronx Supreme with an affidavit from the attorney scheduled to try the case attesting his engagement in another county. "What law school are you in?" the small, thin judge asked. Listening, he wrote the following: I hereby give Jim Smith of St. John's Law School permission to select a jury. "Okay, Son, go pick," he said without humor.

Today you have to struggle through rounds of alternative dispute resolution (ADR) before you ever contemplate a juror. The moment an answer is filed, I'm in some clueless mediator's office figuring a way to say no without screaming the usual curses I learned as a tot on Brooklyn streets. Whole industries have arisen with retired judges dispensing economic sense, patiently and successfully convincing both sides that resolution is best. "All's well that ends," is Judge Marsha Steinhardt's logic, which, it appears, has been adopted nationwide.

Honestly, it's not all bad. It's efficient, cheaper, and maybe even fairer for cases to settle. I learned early that losing is no fun. If you lost at three-on-three in Holy Name schoolyard, you sat for 40 minutes or so until it was your turn again. Hearing the forewoman rule for your unctuous adversary is much worse—it costs money, injures pride, ruins reputation, and causes night terrors. Sometimes the bad guy wins.

But there will come a day—probably after you've assured that client "Yeah, it'll settle," when you're in a courtroom heavy with stale air. Adrenalin flowing, notes on podium, witness sworn, the judge will finally mutter, "You may proceed, Counselor." Here are thoughts on how to be ready for that increasingly rare but almost inevitable day.

Know your subject. Whether crossing an obstetrician, economist, or engineer, master the subject. Don't allow an expert to educate the jury and make you look like a moron. If you haven't learned the intricacies on how stock options are valued, you'll get hurt, and the cross won't work. An experienced expert will eat you alive: "No, Sir, that's incorrect. Let me explain again about how we designed and developed the electronic throttle control system on our Toyotas."

Memorize the facts, the witnesses, and even the law. It's a piece of cake for someone of your skill and intelligence.

Mastering really technical facts and skills is a bigger problem. Learning how to fly a Bombardier Q400, to perform bypass surgery, or to program computer software is hard. We're lawyers, studying hearsay exceptions, deciphering Rube Goldberg cases like *Palsgraf*. We don't make or grow things. We think, speak, and write. Those aren't bad abilities, but we're not designing the iPad or explaining why Pluto's been booted from the list of planets.

Stand in the OR while the surgeon performs his magic, sit in the simulator as the check airman tests a pilot, listen as one of these brilliant nerds explains how apps are created. Obviously, you can't do all in a $50,000 case, but do as much as possible. When I first started handling medical malpractice cases, I read medical texts for an hour or two each day. I would write the unfamiliar terms in a book, look up and study their definitions—something I didn't do for the SATs. Eventually, even I became familiar with the lingo and concepts. Today there's the Internet and it's instant wonder. Use it. Instead of stalking others on Facebook, study. Begin on day one so you'll be effective at depositions, more discerning when hiring experts, more knowledgeable in evaluating your case.

Prepare thoroughly. Very few can cross effectively without extensive preparation. Plan for all the outcomes you can imagine. What if he says "Yes" instead of "No"? What the heck do I do if he agrees? Consider all possibilities.

Compose an outline of objectives. What do I want this witness to say? What direct testimony has hurt me and how can I disprove that information? How will this witness's testimony fit my overall strategy and themes? Have a plan, a goal. Focus on a few critical points: perhaps qualifications—"You've spent your career flying Boeing planes, not the Airbus A340 which was involved in this crash, correct?" Bias—"You know Mr. Jones, true? You've gone to his house? Had dinner? Coffee? He's a friend isn't he?" Lack of actual knowledge—see *My Cousin Vinny*:

Gambini: Is it possible that the two defendants went into the Sac-O-Suds, picked 22 specific items off of the shelf, had the clerk take the money, make change, then leave. Then two different men, drive up . . . in a similar-looking car, go into the store, shoot the clerk, rob him, then leave?

Tipton: No. They didn't have enough time.

Gambini: Why not? How long was they in the store for?

Tipton: Five minutes.

Gambini: Five minutes? How do you know? Did you look at your watch?

Tipton: No.

Gambini: Oh, oh, oh, you testified earlier that you saw the boys go into the store, and you had just begun to cook your breakfast and you were just getting ready to eat when you heard the shot.

Tipton: That's right.

Gambini: So, obviously, it takes you five minutes to cook your breakfast.

Tipton: That's right.

Gambini: That's right, so you knew that. You remember what you had?

Tipton: Eggs and grits.

Gambini: Eggs and grits. I like grits, too. How do you cook your grits? Do you like them regular, creamy, or al dente?

Tipton: Just regular, I guess.

Gambini: Regular. Instant grits?

Tipton: No self-respectin' Southerner uses instant grits. I take pride in my grits.

Gambini: So, Mr. Tipton, how could it take you five minutes to cook your grits when it takes the entire grit-eating world 20 minutes?

Tipton: I don't know, I'm a fast cook I guess.

Gambini: I'm sorry I was all the way over here. I couldn't hear you. Did you say you were a fast cook, that's it?

Tipton: Yeah.

Gambini: Are we to believe that boiling water soaks into a grit faster in your kitchen than anywhere else on the face of the earth?

Tipton: I don't know.

Gambini: Well, I guess the laws of physics cease to exist on top of your stove. Were these magic grits? Did you buy them from the same guy who sold Jack his beanstalk beans?

Always ask leading questions and insist on "Yes" or "No" answers.

Q: You indicated to Mr. Nolan that prior to this accident in 2010 you essentially had no medical problems. Is that right?

A: Yes.

Q: You had arthroscopic surgery on your knee in 2008, 2009?

A: Yes.

Q: Your right knee?

A: Yes.

Q: And Dr. Lawrence, he's your orthodontist?

A: Yes.

Q: You had what is called TMJ prior to this accident?

A: Yes.

Q: Causing neck and back pains?

A: Yes.

Q: Dr. Thomas, he's your general practitioner?

A: Yes.

Q: You saw Dr. Thomas in 2004 complaining of pains in your back radiating around your chest?

A: I don't remember.

Q: And you saw him in 2006 complaining of the same kinds of pain?

A: I don't remember.

Q: Did you see him in 2009 complaining about the same kinds of pain?

A: Yes.

Don't let the witness squirm out of a "Yes"/"No"/"I can't answer 'Yes' or 'No'" answer. Most judges will allow the interruption, "Just 'Yes' or 'No'," when the witness starts to ramble. If the witness resists, stop and sweetly tell him, "I'm going to ask you questions that require "Yes"/"No"/"I can't answer 'Yes' or 'No'" responses. Is that fair?"

Q: You're saying that one of the problems with morphine is addiction. Is that correct?

A: Yes. And the reason—I would like to finish my statement.

Q: You can do it on redirect, Doctor.

A: I would like to answer you now. Is that okay?

Q: I would like you to answer my question.

The Court: Doctor, try to answer the question and try not to volunteer.

Keep your questions short and ask one question at a time. Compound questions are confusing. Long, involved questions lose the jury.

Q: And with your husband and yourself together, did you get back on the elevator? Did you take an escalator or did you take the stairs? Where did you go?

A: In a wheelchair into an ambulance.

Not only four questions, but the moron didn't know that the plaintiff was taken from the accident scene in a wheelchair. I just sat there and smiled.

Never ask an open-ended question. Open-ended questions are for direct: "What then happened?" "Why is that your opinion, Professor?" If you ask "Why?" or "How?" on cross, the witness will ramble for hours. And the judge won't help you: "You asked, Counselor. Now continue, Doctor."

Never ask a question to which you don't know the answer. Of course it'll happen. You're on a roll; the poor schlub is agreeing with everything. And then you go for the kill:

Q: And from the time Mr. Resnick was taken in the ambulance to today, two years, eight months, you never contacted him to see how he was doing, did you?

A: I tried. I was so upset that I called my brother who came and took me home. About an hour or so later, we went to Lutheran and tried to see Mr. Resnick. Nurse Eng said it wasn't a good time. I called the nurse's station every few days for an update, and I was so happy when they told me that Mr. Resnick was doing well and was going to go home. I didn't want to call the family since I received a letter from a lawyer telling me he was going to sue me; I think it was from you, Mr. Nolan, a day or so after the accident.

Or:

Q: You were looking straight ahead?

A: Yes.

Q: And then you heard a bang?

A: Yes.

Q: It was after you heard the bang that you looked over to see the crash? (Hoping you're right.)

A: No, I was looking straight ahead and then I saw this car try to beat the light and I thought, What an idiot. He's gonna kill someone.

If you haven't asked a question at a deposition, leave it alone.

Q: You were looking straight ahead?

A: Yes.

Q: And then you heard the bang?

A: Yes.

Q: And the bang was off to your side?

A: Yes.

Stop. Let the jury figure it out. In summation, you can ask them to think about the situation: How could the witness actually see the impact if he was looking straight ahead and the noise was off to the side?

Uncover all facts at depositions. That's why you take them. If you don't know, don't ask. It's a gamble that you'll lose.

Incorporate your cross into the trial strategy. Remember the O.J. Simpson trial? F. Lee Bailey asked the detective a million times, "Did you ever use the n-word?" "No." "Anyone who said you did is a liar?" "Yes." No matter how many times and ways Bailey asked, the cop was adamant. A totally ineffective cross, I thought. This is the great F. Lee Bailey? He's terrible—long pauses, same question over and again. He looked lost. Later the tapes revealed the cop used the n-word as frequently as my daughter uses the f-word. What appeared as a totally ineffective cross was devastating. The detective lied and was caught. After the tape, no one believed a word; his credibility was destroyed. The trial was lost.

Have a plan for each witness that coordinates with your theme. Looking lame at first is perfect if it later ties into a larger strategy, like Bailey's questions. That's why an outline is essential. What can you achieve? Expose weakness and hammer away. No witness will scream, "I give up. You're right, I'm a liar." Instead, raise a doubt or two; emphasize inconsistencies, and the lack of expertise or credibility. These are small superficial cuts that accumulate slowly but eventually prove fatal to your opponent. Accomplish your objectives and sit down. There's always summation.

Know your audience. Not only the judge and jury but witnesses, too. Some judges encourage a harsh cross; others abhor it. Shouting and running amok can be effective, but only if the judge allows it and there's reason to believe the jury will like it. An intimidating style may not work in the genteel South or with a thoughtful jury. In a malpractice case, the plaintiff's attorney was aggressive and insistent, while the defendant was slow and soft-spoken. Before an educated Manhattan jury, theatrics don't trump logic. The defense used understated reason to quell the natural emotion of the death of a young woman. Reading glasses perched on nose, the defense attorney fumbled around and allowed each witness, even the plaintiff's expert, to respond and explain. This put the plaintiff in a quandary. If he machine-gunned short "Yes" or "No" questions, the jury would wonder why he wouldn't allow defense witnesses the same freedom as the hospital's attorney did. This calculated strategy removed much of the emotion and the verdict was less than the settlement offer.

I've tried cases against attorneys with significant physical disabilities, experts in wheelchairs, fact witnesses with severe speech impediments. Adapt. I've tried nonjury cases where the judge wanted a polite cross—"That tone is not necessary, Mr. Nolan." And another where the judge encouraged me: "Doctor, he didn't ask you that question. . . . Strike out the answer. Let's try to be responsive to the questions he asks, and don't give him a lot of information he didn't ask for."

Be yourself. The rules here are generally, but not always, true. They may not be effective for your case or your witness. Do what's best for your situation. Experience is invaluable. Learn by doing, by getting bounced around a few times and then some more. Eventually, you achieve your goals and stumble back to your chair, battered but satisfied. In a courtroom, nobody escapes without absorbing a right uppercut or two. Cross is a battle which you'll survive if you accomplish your objectives. Remember, it's just a part of a larger strategy. It's great fun to destroy the witness but more fun to win the case.

Closing Argument

The spotlight is on. The audience is hushed, anxious. The evidence is in. The witnesses (who never listen and always disappoint) are gone. Now it's time to orate, to persuade, to prove to judge and jury that you have been correct for all the many past weeks.

It's closing argument, time to break the bounds of evidentiary and black-robed restraint, time to jump up and down, rant and rave. Time to make sense of the intellectual and emotional roller coaster the jury has been riding. Time to make the complex simple; time to convince the jury that you're right and that they should decide for you, if not for your client.

Sure, closing arguments are fun. At last, you can dance around the courtroom and perform just like those smooth lawyers in the movies or on TV. The judge has finally shut up, your opposing counsel's whiny objections will be limited, and some of the jurors may even be awake.

But, despite their appeal, closings are not easy. All the facts and evidence must be gathered and placed under the blanket of the law. The subtleties of proof must be explained, the jurors reminded of weeks-old testimony, and important evidence highlighted. The argument must be clear, concise, and persuasive, and if you fail, you lose. In fact, the freedom and emotion of the closing argument can be a trap. Though you can let go, there must be an underlying discipline and attention to detail.

Therefore, whether from fear or ego, you should consider the following when you seek a captivating closing and victory—or at least when you want to give yourself a chance for success.

Plan ahead. Do not accept the old maxim that the jury has decided the case after the opening statement. Start preparation on your closing *before* trial. Develop themes that you will introduce in jury selection and repeat through trial. Remind the jury in closing of these themes and how you have proven them.

Keep notes during trial. Have a separate part of your trial notebook marked "Closings." If your adversary makes a promise in his opening statement that he does not keep, note it and mark it for the closing section. If a witness makes an admission that helps you, mark it with a *C*. At the end of each trial day, compile all the *C* material into the closings section. When testimony is complete, you can then cull what is important and tailor your argument. All the minor inconsistencies and admissions then will be readily accessible. Use them to bludgeon your enemy. But this will only work if you keep notes. During trial, your mind is racing: Where's the witness? Where did I put that important case? Should I ask this or that? If you do not write these down, you will forget. So review all evidence and testimony. List the points you must cover in your outline.

You may be asking yourself: Why all this paper? Why the compulsive behavior? After all, the greats never used paper; they spoke for hours in wonderful, clear paragraphs. If you were so smart, you would have been a hedge-fund gazillionaire. Keep your outline on the desk, lectern, even in your hand. Refer to it when you speak. That is better than forgetting an essential argument because you didn't want your young associate to doubt that you are the second coming of Edward Bennett Williams.

Know what the judge will charge before you close. You must know the exact wording of the instructions and interrogatories that will be given to the jury. You must mold your argument to the law and the jury interrogatories. Use the same definitions in your closing that the judge will give the jury in the charge. Make it seem that when the judge gives the charge, she is echoing and agreeing with your argument.

If the contested issue in the case is proximate cause, emphasize this. Suppose the judge intends to charge proximate cause as: "An act or omission is a proximate cause of an injury if it was a substantial factor in bringing about the injury, that is, if it had such an effect in producing the injury that reasonable people would regard it as a cause of the injury." You should tell the jury that the defendant's actions were "a proximate cause" of the injuries, that the actions were "a substantial factor," that "reasonable people" such as you jurors would agree that those actions caused Jeanne Gomez's fractured leg. Repeat in your closing the words *proximate cause, substantial factor, reasonable people*—the very phrases used by the judge (who is the only person the jurors trust).

Thus:

"The evidence has shown that the negligence of defendant Chase was a substantial factor in Ms. Gomez's injuries. Now let's review that evidence and testimony and let me show you how it was a substantial factor. When I'm finished, I think you will agree that reasonable people will conclude that those negligent actions were a substantial factor. Do you remember the testimony of . . . ?"

Submit these to the judge and mark them as an exhibit. Make a record. If the judge doesn't charge what you want, object. When in doubt, object. Object in the conference, object in writing, object in court on the record. Don't be afraid to object, even if the judge screams, "Mr. Nolan, you have already objected three times. You've made your record. Now, sit down and shut up."

You don't want to lose on appeal because you failed to object to the charge. Browse any volume of appellate decisions; you will find many where the appellate judges took the easy road and dismissed the appeal because of counsel's failure to object—in the right way or at the right time. It is not enough simply to say, "I object." Put on the record exactly what you think should be charged. Insist that the judge make a record of both your objections and of what you want charged. Be persistent, and do not be intimidated.

Your outline must be written—but not read. Your argument must be developed—but not only in your mind and on paper. Someone has to hear it before the jury does. You and others must *listen* to how the argument sounds. Don't mouth the words. Say them aloud. Try the argument in front of your mirror and in your car. What you think, in the silent recesses of your mind, that you will say and what you *actually* say are often totally different. What reads well doesn't necessarily sound good.

Once you have a bit of confidence, practice in front of an audience—your spouse or ordinary people like your jurors. Practice before someone who will be honest and has common sense. This generally excludes your partners—they may be too arrogant and ignorant of the real world (in other words, too much lawyers) to know good from bad. In New York, it's the subway test. If they ride the R train to work, they live in the real world and recognize lawyer jive. Bounce your closing off R-train people. They are the jurors.

Toss out the legalese. The average juror watches *American Idol*, reads the tabloids, roots for da Bears, and has more common sense than the judge does. Speak the language they understand. It is impossible to overestimate how much the sealed environment of college, law school, and years of practice has removed you from how most people talk. What is obvious to you may not be to the jurors.

If you have any doubt whether the jury will understand a word or phrase, practice before someone who did not spend three boring years in law school. Don't use your secretary. Part of her job is lying to you; how many times has she said that you look like you lost weight? Get ordinary people, leading ordinary lives. If three understand without explanation, then you can use it.

Justice Joseph Levine, now retired from the trial court in Brooklyn, tells of another judge who instructed his jury that if they had a question during deliberations, they were to write it on a piece of paper and have the foreperson sign it. Later the note was returned with more than one signature. When questioned, the jurors responded, "Well, you said four persons should sign it." Use only words that *USA Today* would use in its headlines. You may have more education, but they don't teach street smarts at Yale.

Be aggressive and be positive. Tell the jury what you have proven. Put your adversary on the defensive. If you begin defending your client, then you have lost. Use the active voice. "We proved that Dr. Lewis was at fault in the following ways . . . ." Or "We told you that we would prove that Mrs. Dunn was not at fault and that's what we did." Even if your case has weaknesses, don't start by admitting them. Begin strong and positive. You'll have plenty of time to explain concessions during the rest of the closing.

Be confident in summarizing the evidence and the facts. Repeat the key elements of your case. Even though the jury has heard the facts over and over again, go through the essential elements of your case and show how the evidence has proven each. Refer to the testimony, documents, and law that support your argument.

Emphasize the tangible. Wave the contract or the letter in front of the jury. Read such items; enlarge them for all to see. "I told you that I would prove that the Newton Corporation agreed to purchase . . . Exhibit 25 in evidence states as follows . . . Not only does this written contract, signed by the corporation's president, Suzanne Fish, prove the agreement was in effect, but you heard President Fish admit—right there, on the witness stand—that the contract was in effect. Remember when I asked her . . . and she replied . . . That is from page 427 of the trial transcript."

Emphasize all testimony crucial to your case. Use admissions, "Even defendant's own expert, the guy they paid $4,000 to come here to court, admitted that Bill Malone suffers pain when he walks. Even defendant's expert admitted . . . ." Each admission you trumpet is a Mike Tyson left hook to the body. Hammer away until the head falls. Read them, sing them, parade them about. Admissions, like any weaknesses, are to be exploited. Now is not the time to waffle or straddle, to be a Bill Clinton who didn't inhale. You don't have to shout or be sarcastic, but be aggressive, and keep those fists moving.

Another thing: If at all possible, forget subtlety, detail, and nuance. Drop all the niceties that you put in briefs and that delight law school professors. A closing shouldn't have footnotes. Probably jurors won't understand. If they do, it will consume so much of their attention that they will be confused or forget about the rest. Stick with clear, simple ideas. If the closing argument were music, it would be a rock-and-roll record with a 4/4 beat you can dance to.

It wouldn't be a Bach cantata—as lovely as that might be in some other setting.

Use demonstrative evidence. Words are sacred in our profession. Like priests, we use them to preach to client or court, providing advice we tend to believe has an almost spiritual origin. We listen to the confessions of our clients and colleagues whose sins we can resolve (with the help of a friendly jury), if not forgive. It is all words.

But this is a visual society, nurtured by video games, MTV and ESPN. News, sports, tragedy, and death are seen, not read. To ignore this reality, to cling to mere words in closing argument is to tempt boredom if not defeat. Pictures, graphs, and film overshadow words. Use them. Enlarge the key admission in the trial transcript and read along with the jury. Show them that photo of the accident scene one more time. Intersperse your talk with a model of the head to remind the jurors of the reality of the injury.

Credibility is paramount, both for witnesses and for you. In opening, tell the jury what you intend to prove, what the evidence will show. Now closing is the time to remind the jury that you *have* kept your promise; show them that you have been honest and did not exaggerate. Be specific: "In opening, I told you that we would prove that Mr. Tuthill is permanently, profoundly injured, that his mental capacity has been affected. We have proven this—from his testimony, his wife's, his co-workers', his treating doctors', Drs. Masella, Schneider, and Russo. . . ."

It is also the time to remind the jury—if there is a basis for it—that your adversary failed to keep her promise. "You know, jurors, when Mrs. Clancy made her opening statement, she promised to prove three things. I remember because I wrote them down: Just five days ago, she said she would prove (1) that Mr. Cook suffered no out-of-pocket loss of wages and medical bills, (2) that he made a remarkable recovery, and (3) his two shoulder surgeries had nothing to do with his accident. Now, I waited—you probably did too—during all the testimony and documents, waiting to learn if Mrs. Clancy would keep her word. She did not. Even Mrs. Clancy's own expert orthopedist, Dr. Mitchell, agreed that Mr. Cook's two shoulder surgeries were the result of the incident; that the car crash was a proximate cause of those surgeries as well as the pain. . . ."

You must keep your bond with the jury. Lawyers are as highly regarded as cockroaches on the kitchen floor. Do not reinforce this belief by lying. If your adversary does so, ram it down his throat—in a nice way.

A jury must be entertained. During the trial, your ability to do this is limited. The witnesses' testimony is dry and convoluted. Nothing comes out in a logical order. The room is hot and the acoustics are terrible. The lawyers bicker or confer mysteriously with the judge. The jury dreams of being anywhere but in these cramped, uncomfortable seats with the worst people in the world—lawyers.

But closings are—or can be—entertainment. If jurors fall asleep during your closing argument, give up; change professions. Become the accountant that your mother always wanted. An entertaining closing, however, is not always simple. You now have the freedom to raise your voice, to walk about, to slam your fist on the table, to call the plaintiff someone "who thinks this lawsuit is Lotto." But be careful. Don't force the theatrics.

If you are emotional and love to scream and yell, then do. If you are calculating and controlled, then that is your closing. Any decent trial lawyer is both. Learn from others. But do not attempt to be someone else. You are yourself, for good or bad. You will be a competent, intelligent advocate. Like everyone else. Admit it: No one will ever write a book about you. So what if you never move a juror to tears? You will be successful if you work hard, know your file, and be yourself. Of course, it helps if you have a good case. But when in doubt, use your instincts.

Look jurors in the eyes and ask them to give you what you want. Standing cold at a podium reading a closing is not good form. You should have developed a rapport and sense of trust with the jury by the time you get to closing. If you haven't, it's probably too late. To win, you must convince them. If you cannot look each juror in the eye when you ask for $10 million, your verdict will reflect that.

The jurors may know what your goal is during trial. But you must not assume that they do. Tell them exactly what you want; ask them to return a verdict finding no negligence on the part of your client. Or to return a verdict finding negligence against each defendant and awarding $2.3 million. If you don't tell them, how will they know? Be clear and specific. If allowed, blow up the jury interrogatories and complete them with the jury. Fill in how you want them answered. Do not hesitate, and do not be shy.

Thank the jurors and sit down. Good closing arguments are important, of course, but when it is time to stop, do so.

My First Trial

I never wanted to be a lawyer, but I went to law school anyway. After a few years of studying *Palsgraf*, the Uniform Commercial Code, the Rule against Perpetuities, and other otherworldly trivialities, I decided I needed some experience—especially since I had never even been in a law office. I taught high school English and attended law school at night, so one hot summer I volunteered at Legal Services in downtown Brooklyn where I could meet real lawyers, clients, and maybe a black-robed judge or two.

With shoes shined, I climbed the steps to the Legal Services worn and tiny offices and was assigned to assist a soft-spoken lawyer who looked like Al Pacino in *Serpico* without the white mouse. Given a perfunctory nod, I sat and watched as poor, mostly helpless blacks, Hispanics, a few whites told painful tales of cruel landlords and filthy, dilapidated tenements. These heart-wrenching stories nearly made me cry but were met with businesslike questioning from the lawyer. No "How ya doin'?," no "Sorry for your troubles," which were part of my DNA. Simply: "What can I do for you?"

And he didn't help everyone. Some were callously told "Sorry" and dismissed with a wave. If he could help, he'd fill out a form and send the weary client to another who would hear the entire lament and begin the paperwork to fight the evil, ruthless landlord in filthy, dilapidated Civil Court a few blocks away.

109

I learned to complete the forms and was allowed to view the zoo that was the Landlord/Tenant Part: It was like a legal bazaar, with lawyers shouting names, cutting deals, signing stipulations until the judge arrived with a bunch of court officers and proceeded to try to quiet the throng. Some judges were polite and tolerant of the buzz emanating from the hundreds who jammed the giant courtroom. Others were like lion tamers minus the whip. "Quiet!" they screamed. "I said quiet!" "Take off your hats. This is a courtroom." "You, Sir, remove your hat now or I'll have you tossed out." "You picking your nose, stop it. That's right." After all, this was Brooklyn in the mid-1970s, all elbows and simmering heat which would erupt next July during a blackout when whole neighborhoods were looted and torched.

For me it was pure excitement, constant action with hundreds of cases on every day. Landlord lawyers, arms loaded with files, would demand eviction; the tenant lawyer would beg for a few months of mercy. The judge would instantly rule and move to the next poor slob.

The people in this world spoke an alien language that all understood except me and the few innocent souls who believed justice would prevail when they politely explained why the rent was overdue. "You have a lawyer?" the judge would demand. "Why don't we put this over for two weeks so you can get a lawyer. Next."

No cases were cited; the law, rarely. Not exactly how we were taught in quiet classrooms. The real world was noisy, crowded, chaotic—a hulking, massive beast where each case was decided in seconds; no time for contemplation, reflection, analysis. Lawyers handled 10, 20 cases at once, juggling files, scurrying to various courtrooms, tossing dimes into payphones, stopping only to scrape and bow when a judge strolled by.

After a week or so of mostly observing, I was assigned a case. An elderly, proper woman with a Scandinavian accent told me that her husband, with whom she didn't live, was evicted while he was an inpatient at Methodist Hospital even though the rent was paid. When I met her, the Judgment of Eviction had been entered and her husband's clothes and furniture, she maintained, were piled on the sidewalk.

Ridiculous. Who would toss an old, sick man onto the bitter concrete? And commit fraud by affirming that the rent was delinquent? Such malice exists only in the imagination.

We piled into my battered Volkswagen Bug and drove to the shabby brownstone off 7th Avenue in Park Slope to find bags of clothes and some decrepit furniture piled near the curb. It's not like I was a rube from Peoria or Dubuque—I was "brung up" in Brooklyn, as we say—but I was shocked and shaken. And I was told the same sad story at bedside by William Schaefer: how he lived alone in the apartment for years, always paid his rent, and didn't even know about the eviction until his wife went to pick up his mail and found the papers taped to his door.

I hurried to the office and eagerly prepared—with assistance—an Order to Show Cause and other documents to overturn the eviction and reinstate my client. Since I was part of the Legal Services' summer program, I could act as an admitted lawyer—appear in court, argue motions, try cases. So I pleaded with some cynical judge that the eviction be overturned and silently steamed while the landlord's attorney gave a million reasons for the eviction. As I recall some 35 years later, we were in court one or two more times, pressed to settle the matter, until the judge gave up and assigned a date for a nonjury trial.

I don't remember being nervous as I sat with this odd couple— married 30 years before, lived together only a few months, never divorced. I had never even seen a trial, so I just reviewed the facts and told them to tell the truth. How hard could it be?

My adversary was a heavy, pleasant fellow who spent his life representing landlords. Perpetually frenzied, he was interested in a fee, not justice. When they don't pay, we evict them. That's what I get paid for. Whaddya expect? Right and wrong never entered his mind.

I'm sure an offer was made for my client to vacate since he was paying peanuts and the rent could be doubled for a new tenant. Indeed, the landlord leased the apartment to someone else as soon as the Judgment of Eviction was issued. With my client having nowhere to live, this was summarily rejected.

We were assigned to Gaspar Fasullo, an older, amiable judge who was quietly reading the paper as we entered. The small, drab courtroom was empty except for the clerk, my clients, and the landlord, a small, older gentleman in a suit and tie and holding a hat that went out of style in the early 1960s. Certainly, this grandfather type wasn't the malevolent ogre I had imagined.

In my most serious voice, I opened and told a tale of outrage and illegality. My adversary was more measured, describing a pattern of late payments and detailing the legalities of the eviction. I called my client and began to ask about living on Sterling Place. During the direct, Mr. Schaefer wandered, discussing events of years ago or his illnesses. He talked about everything except the eviction.

"Isn't it true that the landlord knew you were in Methodist Hospital?"

"Objection, leading."

"Sustained."

I had no idea what that meant so I continued:

"Your landlord was aware you were in Methodist, isn't that right?"

"Objection, leading."

"Sustained."

"Even though you paid the rent, you were still evicted?"

"Sustained," the judge said without prompting.

I continued with nearly every question met with "Objection, leading," until eventually, with the judge's assistance, I wrestled the narrative from my unsophisticated, befuddled client.

The first question on cross from my adversary was:

"Isn't it a fact that you didn't pay rent for two months?"

"Objection," I stormed. "Leading."

"No, no," the judge laughed. "On cross he can lead; on direct you can't lead."

Who knew? I then realized my law school education was worthless in a courtroom.

My adversary, not exactly Clarence Darrow, damaged my client's credibility, and for the first time, I realized that I could lose. I was panicking.

Mrs. Schaefer took the stand and I asked a few open-ended questions and shut up. Articulate and sympathetic, she told of their unusual yet simple lives. Immigrating to Brooklyn, marrying but never consummating the relationship, working at menial jobs, and how she cared for him as his health deteriorated. A fascinating saga of real love, not the fleeting romantic kind, but the long-term love of another. One grown old and ill could easily be ignored. Instead, she stepped into his life with compassion and without complaint.

Her goodness and benevolent demeanor didn't spare the landlord her wrath. And the judge loved it. My cross of the landlord was somewhat effective or at least that's what I was told by one of the Legal Services lawyers who stopped by. During summation, I was emboldened with indignation and sarcasm. I have to say, even with 30-plus years perspective, I went way over the top.

A week or two later, on August 13, 1976, Judge Fasullo ruled that the landlord "without cause or justification, wrongfully, unlawfully and illegally took possession" of my client's apartment and reinstated him as of August 31. In addition, my client was awarded legal fees of $125, which, I was told, was extremely rare and for which I was congratulated. I hoped the meager amount was not a reflection of my ability.

The summer soon ended and I returned to teaching and law school. I had stumbled upon a vocation, having enjoyed all aspects of the trial, even the pathetic landlord who couldn't comprehend his own immorality. I relished the give-and-take, the direct and cross, and the closing.

Back then, I knew it all. After all, I was 26. Yet I had experienced a heartless world, inhabited by greedy landlords and cheating tenants, where justice occurs rarely. Happy endings, I realized, were fleeting, since Mr. Schaefer died shortly after returning to his home.

Yet, I still smile when I recall the words and face of the landlord, whom I ran into a few months later when he recognized me and spit, "You really screwed me up, you know that?"

A Brand New World

We lived on farms, then we lived in cities, and now
we're going to live on the internet.

—*The Social Network*

We don't talk. We text, tweet, e-mail, and post the mundane
and forgettable—"little Zoe slept till 8:30, big lax game tomorrow,
omg the best pepperoni pizza." We publicize unimportant, trivial
incidents that reveal our lives to be painfully ordinary.

The young are addicted to these amazing instruments. As a result, they talk less, interact less, date less. Everything is visual. Words
have little value. A penny, a good old copper Abe for each smiley-
face emoticon, would make me as rich as Mark Zuckerberg. Words
no longer express emotions; symbols convey sadness, humor, or
love.

Spelling rules, once inviolate, are obsolete. Words are short-
ened, abbreviated for speed, and space is more important than accuracy. And don't just tell me about the seafood risotto at the hip
East Village Italian, here's a picture. If you want to learn about the
sleek bar and ancient bathroom, check out the video on my
Facebook page. Words are inadequate, take too long, require too
much thought and effort. Just browse the photos and videos and
you'll see everything.

115

This new, less verbal, more visual, more shallow and rushed world has even invaded the traditional ornate courtrooms where serious disputes are decided. Even an ancient codger like me can't fathom how we communicated years ago when we threw coins into phones. How we cursed, with blood pressure exploding, when the phone booth was occupied or dimes ran out. How we called the office once or maybe twice a day while traveling to check on our messages. How the "While You Were Out" notes piled up. How everything took so long, from doing research to typing a brief to filing a motion.

Fortunately, those days are past, yet speed and ease have a cost. Some contend—yeah, I'm one—we have lost an ability to contemplate, to listen, to converse, to argue in a coherent manner. The mania to demonize or venerate Sarah Palin's every word, the reckless posting of cruel words and vulgar photos are emblematic of this age of detached immediacy.

But no trial lawyer can just bemoan or regret. These inclinations may be unfortunate, but the people who have them are our jurors—some now, all 10 years from now. Their addiction to immediacy and their ability to research parties, facts, medical and scientific opinions present new problems for those who try cases. We're arguing before those who, by age 21, have spent triple the time playing virtual games than reading; whose access to people, information, and thought is a click away. The practice of waiting until morning to learn the Cubbies' losing score, of waiting until school to reveal the latest gossip—actually, of waiting for anything—is long gone.

Even we, who still wear suits and ties, must adapt. To succeed, we must persuade our audience, those half-dozen or so taxpaying neighbors who vow to be fair. Yet these younger citizens are not used to or content with piecemeal information. A simple scan of a Facebook profile reveals interests, relationships, education, family—more than even the most determined stalker would crave. Not only are they used to massive amounts of data, but they are adept at uncovering the most minute details in relative seconds. We must be realistic and admit that, despite Her Honor's admonitions, some jurors will head to Google and perhaps unearth more about the lawsuit during lunch on an iPhone than is provided in weeks of testimony. And they will be more influenced by what they read on a blog than by any insightful reasoning.

Indeed, one lawyer, scheduled for trial, deleted any Twitter or Facebook post that was even remotely political or controversial. He reasoned that the jurors, despite the judge's instructions, would search the Net about the lawsuit and its lawyers. He didn't want any of his political views to antagonize a juror. He feared that if a juror disagreed, the juror would allow those differences to influence how he judged the case.

It's a new world, and it changes each moment. What the young expect is much different than it was for my generation, which grew up with newspapers, seven TV channels, and hand-written love letters. Trial strategy must include what jurors want and must take into account how they absorb testimony and evidence. Some Neanderthals are loathe to alter a winning (or even a losing) formula. You'll have to adapt. Here are some pointers on doing that.

Use the Internet

And not just for reading *Above the Law*. Knowing your case means more than memorizing facts, witness statements, and scientific terms. Google your client, experts, adversary, witnesses, and judge. If you're unsure about how to do this, have a teenager assist. She'll probably be able to pull up your grades from high school. And don't forget the blogs. Even a mundane two-car collision should be researched. It's easy to view the intersection on Google Street View. Discover information on the driver and the owner. You never know what'll turn up.

Indeed, some lawyers Facebook potential jurors, searching for personal details such as TV preferences, friends, and any interests which may reveal empathy toward a side. I warn clients not to post anything about their claims, and you know that video of you dancing on the bar, don't you think you should delete it? As soon as the defendant smells potential liability, extensive Internet research is commenced. Posting innocuous statements such as "I feel terrif" or "I'm soooo happy" may be fodder for cross-examination if damages include medical or emotional harm.

Don't get me wrong. Having fun is in my genes. Some of the best laughs have been at wakes and after funerals. But as Rooney

Mara said in *The Social Network*: "The Internet's not written in pencil, Mark, it's written in ink."

In this new era, how and when do you provide your most effective witnesses and evidence? Do you frontload crucial documentation to satisfy digital-age impatience? Do you build suspense by slowly adding piece by piece? It depends, of course, on your case, your style, and your audience. But consider all options before embarking. Do you address criticism, no matter how misplaced, listed on a blog? Do you respond on the Net, in the courtroom, or both? Neither? There's no set answer to these new and perplexing issues. But learn what's on the Net so you can consider some type of response in planning your trial strategy.

As in all trial work, no rigid formulas apply, but it is a given that the Net and its power add a new dimension to our practice. It's now much easier to determine the value of an injury. One personal injury blog in New York City details how the incident occurred, lists verdicts with each item of damages specified, analyzes decisions on appeal all with photos, medical descriptions, and illustrations. A half-hour search can provide numerous examples of the value of leg injuries, which include biographical information on the plaintiff, types and number of surgeries, and the extent of medical treatment and rehabilitation. And this blog is not unique. Should you pray that no juror stumbles across this site as you demand double that amount? Or do you make reference to it during trial? Without specifically mentioning the Internet statement, I would distinguish between what is written on the blog and the facts of the case on trial.

The days of blow-ups of hospital charts, fumbling around with fuzzy X-rays, and writing on a blackboard are so Middle Ages. Demonstrative evidence must be interactive and sophisticated. It's relatively inexpensive to use deposition excerpts, videos, PowerPoints, and animations. Years ago, we made a 20-minute *Day in the Life* video of a handicapped young child. Our pleas for more money were mocked by the crotchety old judge who was trying to settle the case. After viewing the tape for a few minutes, the judge turned to the defendant: "You have to pay more."

Use animation to show the accident, to explain the manufacturing process, or to make the complex clear. Perception is reality, so spend as much time on how evidence is presented as on accumulating it. You're not going to win if jurors can't comprehend your evidence, and jurors these days comprehend differently.

Traditionally, experts and other witnesses would provide substantial oral testimony augmented by a visual aid or two. Today, testimony should be primarily interactive with oral testimony only necessary to introduce and explain what is shown to the jury.

Our image of an ideal attorney is one of righteous oratory—Atticus standing proud, proving the innocence of Tom Robinson. It is the words we admire, the universal and gracious rhetoric that draws us to this profession. It is not some geek in scuffed shoes clicking a button to start an animation that has jurors nodding and smiling because now they understand everything. Unfortunately, those guys with scuffed shoes are taking over, and mere words aren't what they used to be.

Soon, our entire audience will be those addicted to the visual. Words will have less import and influence. Oh, sure, there will be times—motions or appeals—when argument is essential, when we can exhibit the skill which attracted us to this still noble calling. Yet to pretend that words alone, no matter how compelling, can triumph over an entertaining and enlightening video is to deny reality. Remember, Atticus's most persuasive moment is when Tom stands and shows the jury his withered left arm.

The Client's Suffering

Initially, it's anger.

Anger at the airline for running out of fuel, crashing onto a hill, tearing the four-month-old child from his mother's arms to his death. The mother, whose injured left arm was rendered useless, sadly survived, tormented by incessant demons and inexplicable guilt, unable to share them with anyone, including her husband.

Or anger at the drunk driver with the 24 previous license suspensions who runs a red light at 70 mph without headlights, dragging and mutilating a mother and her two teenage girls to horrific deaths. The perfect family is destroyed. The father, injured as well, talks of wishing to die except for the needs of his teenage son. In a home filled with family and graduation photos, he reminds you that his daughters were active in Students Against Drunk Driving. The house and its cruel reminders of the once bright future will have to be sold. Between tears, he curses the driver to a slow death.

Sometimes it's not only anger: It's depression, apathy, or a combination of emotions. It's always, however, tragedy, permanent heart-searing tragedy. Death. Paralysis. Brain damage. Amputation. From plane crashes, or car accidents, or medical malpractice, or defective products. The kind you read about, the kind you see paraded on TV, the kind you pray you never experience. The crown of thorns that some must endure in this life.

But you are the lawyer. You know the damage can never be altered. You know the client and family look to you for assistance, for guidance, and, occasionally, for unattainable revenge. Your job is to counsel, to explain, and to litigate.

Emotionally, you empathize with their troubles. You yearn to make the person and the family whole again. Legally, you want to right the wrong, eradicating financial worry for this family, changing their lives and allowing them to move from the tenement to the sunny respectability of a house and pool in Arizona.

But, truth be told, not all your thoughts are so noble. Late at night when you are alone, you even admit to yourself that some ego is involved. After all, this is the case that you have been seeking, the one you have deserved but until now has eluded you. This is the case that will pay college tuitions, purchase that summer home in Nantucket, put your face on the six o'clock news, and prove to others what you already knew—that you are the equal (if not the better) of your colleagues whose names are household words. Once this case is won, your name will be added to that number. The bar lecture circuit will come begging, and your war stories will be the talk of cocktail parties. Then judges will seek your counsel, and young trial lawyers in waiting will laugh at your jokes.

For the catastrophic, media-grabbing case with the sympathetic family appears, at outset, an easy victory. But be careful. Without diligent work and effective strategy, the result could be disastrous not only to your client but also to your career. Don't let it happen.

A case of this magnitude evokes the best and the worst of your personality: the sympathetic, caring side that your mother (but no one else, especially your spouse and partners) sees, and the dark side, formed by the greed, hubris, and cynicism that you have acquired in the years since law school. These two sides will compete through the litigation, as you decide whether to settle or to try, to value the case honestly, or to allow your client to dream in a world of multimillion-dollar headlines.

And this internal conflict isn't the only problem. The pressure is on. The family and the community expect Lotto results. "If a woman can recover $2.9 million for spilling some McDonald's coffee on herself . . . ." The courthouse regulars are already jealously critiquing your strategy. And your partners are busily spending your fee before the lawsuit has been filed.

Even worse, while the expectations of your client and your partners become more unrealistic, the opposition has entirely different ideas: They are gearing up. The experienced defendants do not panic. Instead, they retain top guns. And they are ready to fight, not only for the millions at risk but also for the reputation of the product and, perhaps, the continued existence of the corporation.

And so, even though your client will naturally evoke as much sympathy as any juror can provide, you have enormous work ahead. To defeat your formidable adversaries, fulfill your dreams, justify your ego, satisfy your partners, and serve and comfort your client, you must do the following:

First, take the case seriously. You will be tempted to rely too much on the client's gruesome injuries or on the tears of the widow and her children, and convince yourself that the defendants will be paralyzed by fear of a runaway verdict. They will throw money at you to settle. No jury, you believe, can ever look at this wheelchair and mutter, "Defendant's verdict," or even "$600,000." The sympathy is almost unbearable: $5 million, $10 million maybe, but nothing less. Incomprehensible, you think. Impossible, you are told.

Don't believe it. Don't delude yourself. The defendants are cornered and their attorneys will battle to save their clients' assets and reputation. Instead of rolling over, defendants will spend more, work harder, and explore every aspect of the case. You never know what that 10-year-old medical record will reveal, what the victim's high school records will illuminate, or what a co-worker will expose.

The defendants will use all resources to prevent the $25 million verdict, the punitive damages, the newspaper and Internet headlines that will send their stock spiraling. Just as your reputation is at stake, so is the defense attorney's. With a victory in a case that seems impossible to win, the professional and financial rewards garnered by defense counsel are immense—especially because their insurer or corporation always has more business, and can always refer another lucrative case.

To obtain the handsome result your client deserves, your mindset must be on work, not on glory. Preparation must start immediately, and you must prepare, not for settlement, but for trial.

Investigation must be commenced, legal research performed, documents obtained, experts hired. Money must be spent and clients counseled.

Some tasks can be delegated. The essential ones, however, you must do yourself. Master the facts, the clients, the witnesses, the law. Complete and thorough knowledge of everything is paramount. Remember that the defense has more resources, and often more people, since there are usually numerous defendants and therefore several defense attorneys, each of whom has an insurance adjuster looking over her shoulder.

If the case is prepared with the false hope of settlement, maximum recovery will not result. Defendants and their principals are not nice guys. To pay as little as possible, every tactic will be deployed, and the ethical envelope will be pushed. Every weakness in your case will be exploited. In the hardball world of million-dollar injury and death cases, most defendants respond to nothing less than a foot on the neck. Only the strength that comes from preparation for trial will enable you to do that.

Trusting the other side is a luxury you cannot afford. Unless you are certain through experience of your opponent's integrity, take no chances. Maintain a healthy amount of New York City paranoia: Trust no one all the time. You remember how it was in childhood: "You don't mind if I get that in writing, do you, Mom?"

To handle the case effectively, you must know your clients. In the ordinary injury case, you may meet the client when you are retained and once or twice after that, before depositions and then before trial. Younger partners and associates can fill in the gaps.

In a huge case, this is inadequate. Since the emotional loss is much greater, meet with the client, her family and close friends regularly to sustain your relationship and to understand their needs and desires. Become involved in their lives and learn their fears, their hopes, and their histories. Do this to nurture them emotionally, to gain their trust, and to know them. After one of my partners settled a case involving the death of a teenager, the mother told him: "I want to thank you for saving my husband's life." And she meant that literally. Sometimes the emotional component of your representation outweighs the legal.

Any competent defense lawyer will insist on obtaining all the relevant documents, will interview dozens of co-workers, and will perform extensive surveillance on an injured plaintiff. Because the defendants will read every record—medical, financial, school, and work—and surf the Net, you must learn more. Visit your clients' homes; talk with their friends and relatives. Learn the good and bad. Open those skeleton-filled closets and take a long, hard look inside. Be skeptical. Ask probing questions about the marriage and the job. Ask embarrassing questions about that arrest for DUI. In short, learn everything.

Then investigate, if for no other reason than to rule out any problem during discovery. You don't need a surprise at trial. If something bad exists, find it and deal with it. Pretending it won't be discovered is naïve.

If there is a problem with law enforcement, for example, learning about it early will enable you to minimize it. Having it thrust upon you later—at deposition or trial—can be devastating. In one death action, defense counsel sent a young associate to rummage through our client's hundreds of cancelled checks. Each unknown payee was tracked down; one was traced to a marriage counselor. Although it turned out to be rather innocuous, the defense argued that the marriage was not the bed of roses we suggested. Diligence is an asset that can translate into savings for the defense. The only way to combat that is to be more thorough.

Determine who pulls the strings for your client and his family. People who have suffered loss usually look to others for advice. In educated families, a parent, uncle, or cousin might provide financial guidance. In uneducated families, someone outside the family, perhaps someone who has more education or a position of power in the community, might help make important decisions. Learn the string-pullers' motivations. If their goals are selfish or corrupt, confront these influences. And, regardless, knowing who is making the call will provide insight into the goals and desires of your client.

A continual battle will be fought during litigation between what the facts are and what your client is told by "well-meaning" friends. The more you are with your client, the more you build rapport and the ability to help your client distinguish truth from fiction.

Where you bring the action often determines whether you win—and if you do, how much you collect. Plaintiffs prefer state courts in urban areas. Juries and judges are more liberal. Defendants prefer federal courts in conservative jurisdictions. There, discovery is usually broader, the judges—usually from large firms that represent corporate America—are more sympathetic to the defense, and the jury pool will include the suburban or rural conservative juror.

The law is often secondary. Juror inclinations can be much more significant. Generally, an Idaho jury with liberal wrongful death law will award less than a Bronx jury with conservative New York wrongful death law. A suburban Georgia jury will award your client less than an urban Miami jury.

Of course, there are exceptions. In the *Pan Am/Lockerbie* trial, for example, a white juror from the suburbs assumed the role of Henry Fonda in *12 Angry Men,* convincing a divided jury to decide in favor of the plaintiffs, while two black elderly women from the city, clutching their Bibles, were the last holdouts for the defense. You never know for sure. All you can do is rely on your instincts.

Is precedent favorable to a finding of fault on your theory? Enumerate the items of damages, particularly in death actions where some states allow recovery for grief and loss of affection, while others permit recovery only for pecuniary loss. Learn the law of all potential jurisdictions before venue is selected. If a plane crashes in Indiana and the defendants include a joint Italian/French manufacturer and an air carrier that is incorporated in Delaware, has its principal place of business in Virginia, and is a wholly owned subsidiary of a Delaware corporation with a principal place of business in Texas, where do you bring suit if your client is an English citizen with a green card, teaching in Montreal, whose wife is from California, teaching in Indiana, but thinks of New York as a home?

And once you choose venue, what liability law will be applied? What damage law? Is it the law of Indiana on liability, and the law of Quebec on damages, determined by a Texas jury? Is the foreign manufacturer entitled to a nonjury trial pursuant to the Foreign Sovereign Immunities Act? Can the case be kept in state court? You must know the answers to practice the art of forum shopping.

Substantive law and the history of jury awards in the locale are not the only considerations; tort reform and its effects must be evaluated as well. Are there caps on non-economic damages? In a case involving a victim without dependents, such as an infant, the loss of society and the grief of the survivors define the damages. There is little, if any, economic loss. Therefore, a jurisdiction with a cap on such items will be disastrous.

Learn everything. Master the intricacies of the product or procedure that is the basis of the claim. In an obstetrical medical malpractice case: when to use Pitocin, the differences between internal and external fetal monitors. Read the texts, purchase a set of forceps. Find all publications by government oversight agencies. Obtain any standards set by national associations, such as the American College of Obstetricians and Gynecologists. These standards are often changed periodically, so make sure that the edition that you have was in effect on the date of the malpractice. Then mark the standards as an exhibit at the defendant doctor's deposition, and cross her on whether they were followed during the labor and delivery. If not, watch her squirm to justify her noncompliance.

Research the product. Search for similar incidents. Interview current and former employees of the retailer or manufacturer. A disgruntled former employee can be the gold you're seeking.

Begin your investigation as soon as you are retained. I was once called by a friend who told of a 55-year-old who went to the emergency room with chest pains. Instead of being admitted or observed, he was diagnosed as having heartburn, given Mylanta, and discharged. That evening he died of a heart attack. The family rightfully believed that he should have been admitted. Because I feared that the emergency room EKG tracing would disappear, I immediately went to the hospital to secure the records. While there, a young resident, call her Dr. Pesce, pulled me aside and told me that she was the physician who examined the victim and discharged him. When I eventually obtained the hospital record, the name of the examining physician was illegible. The formal response to my demand for the names of all physicians in the emergency room did not include Dr. Pesce. And at depositions, no one knew who had treated the plaintiff in the hectic emergency room. If I had not immediately run to the hospital, I would have never been able to question the physician who was responsible for the treatment. Speed is essential.

You must find the best experts. Hire them early and often. No one is as knowledgeable as the surgeon or the mechanic or the crane operator who devotes his life to a daily routine. If the plane crash involved ice on the wing, hire a meteorologist to analyze the weather pattern, warnings, and technology available to predict the problem. Hire a pilot who flies the particular type of plane involved to provide you with his experience and training, and the "hangar talk" among similar pilots. Hire a former NTSB investigator to provide insight into the cause of the crash and to analyze any government findings. Hire an ex–air traffic controller to tell you whether the plane was properly held in the air and whether any procedures were disobeyed. The list goes on. Select those experts who will educate you. You need not use them at trial, but it's always better to have more than less. In the catastrophic case, you must spend money. Effective experts are not cheap but should prove their worth.

Initially, you need experts to advise you of not only the strengths but the weaknesses of your case. Maybe the expert is not articulate and does not look like Brad Pitt, but use him during discovery to educate you, prepare you for depositions, and interpret documents. If the expert is qualified and will devote time to educating you, then he is valuable regardless of whether he will ultimately testify. At trial, however, the appearance and jury appeal of an expert are important. Experts must teach jurors and must translate scientific lingo into everyday language. On cross, experts cannot afford to become angry or disconcerted. An experienced expert never becomes combative or flustered, no matter how heated the cross: "Doctor, isn't it true that you've testified 20 times this year, in similar cases, all for plaintiffs, never for a hospital or doctor?" Turning to the jury, he smiles sweetly and replies with a confident "Yes."

Pedigree and education are important, but real hands-on experience is paramount. The truck driver, the 777 pilot, the machine press operator are impressive—especially in uniform with lapels or in grease-stained overalls. Of course, star quality is a real plus. Try cross-examining an astronaut who walked on the moon about his testimony that the pilot of a 737 that crashed was not at fault. In a trial where that happened, even the judge was excited and had his photo taken with this hired gun.

Be open to resolution at any time. Obtain client authority for a demand. But be patient if your client is unreasonable early on. Any competent defense attorney or insurance adjuster will understand if you respond "$100 million." Let your client's anger subside during the litigation. Usually, the demand will become more reasonable.

Examine your client's financial needs and find out whether a slightly smaller settlement early in the case might be financially advantageous. Consider structured settlements if your client is financially unsophisticated. Do not let your ego intrude on what should be a business decision in your client's best interest. Communicate offers in writing and likewise confirm their rejection if you believe that the jury will award less.

Without a settlement, this will be a shootout, the championship fight, the clash of the titans. Like all battles, it begins with preparation. As you walk through the courthouse door, have your papers ready on the legal issues and the scientific issues. Educate the judge and her law clerk. The first pages of your scientific brief should be a glossary. Is an aileron something from outer space? Define the technical terms, use illustrations or photos to make the difficult simple. Remember, the judge spends most of her time either on slip-and-fall cases or on drug cases. It is rewarding when the judge thumbs through your brief while the expert testifies.

Make your motions in limine before jury selection so that you know what is admissible. This is especially true for demonstrative evidence. Do not focus your case around a video re-creation of the accident only to have the judge rule in the middle of trial that it is inadmissible. Have the judge rule before you open, so you can adapt your strategy, witnesses, and proof.

Use a shadow or mock jury. You have immersed your life in this action. You know more about myocardial biopsies than the chief of cardiology at Einstein Medical Center, your children call you the "heart doctor daddy," and your partners seek advice on their cardiac problems. But your immersion in the facts and technical medical issues may skew how you communicate them—or even how you understand them. A run-through of your evidence and argument before one or more mock juries may surprise you and may color your judgment about what is effective. Have professional jury consultants organize these mock trials. But be sure to use jurors from the jurisdiction as the jury pool.

During trial, remember jurors are suspicious of lawyers—especially plaintiff's lawyers. They believe you're a shyster. Convince them otherwise. Either in jury selection or opening, establish rapport. It is always better to address jurors during jury selection. But if the questioning of jurors is not permitted, try to establish a connection with jurors in your opening. Admit weaknesses. Inform them of the warts—the messy divorce, the drug bust, the history of heart disease. Be honest. Discuss sympathy before the defendant uses it as a club. Tell them that justice, not sympathy, is your goal and their responsibility.

Always understate damages. A momentary view of a brain-damaged infant is infinitely more articulate and persuasive than your 15-minute description. A mother sitting with her children alone on a wooden bench shouts volumes. Let witnesses describe the 65 seconds of terror as the plane plunged to earth, the lack of any appreciable remains, the nightmares, the loneliness, the fear of raising a family alone.

Do not have your severely injured client in the courtroom every day. With familiarity comes callousness. A few appearances are sufficient.

Timing of witnesses is important. By establishing liability first, you will gain the jurors' trust. They will understand that you are not relying on sympathy to establish your case.

Then proceed to damages. Use experts to establish cost of medical and custodial care. Ask the doctor how many times a week your client must be treated by a therapist and for how long. Have the doctor testify about the daily cost of such services. Bring in a therapist or a rehabilitation expert to discuss specific amounts.

Be conservative with your numbers. Do not destroy your economist's credibility by having him testify to projections without support or foundation. When you estimate the lost earnings of a disabled infant, the real numbers are astronomical enough to shock the juror scraping by on $50,000 a year. Do not endanger your credibility by trying for that extra $200,000.

Use demonstrative evidence: photos, graphs, videos, PowerPoints, blow-ups—whatever works. But, again, be a minimalist. Too much is a turnoff. Keep the *Day in the Life* film to less than 20 minutes. Let experts use demonstrative evidence to teach, to highlight, to convince. We are a visual generation, raised on film and television. The technology is there—use it.

Your client should testify. Keep it short and to the point. Avoid dramatics. With any significant loss, tears flow without prompting. Have other relatives, friends, the boss confirm what a great mother, wife, teacher, the victim is or was. Again, keep testimony brief. But be sure to have a few individuals who have no interest in the outcome testify to emphasize the goodness, the beauty, the joy that has been lost forever.

In closing, be assured. Look the jurors in the eyes and tell them what you want in language they understand. Do not be apologetic if you ask for an amount that the jurors will collectively never earn in their lifetimes. If you hesitate, it will be perceived as lack of conviction. If you don't believe in your case, why should the jury? Refer to the exact language on the jury questionnaire so the jurors understand how the questions should be answered. But always remind them that the final determination is theirs.

Finally: Wait for the jury's decision with the quiet confidence of someone who has done his job well. If you have worked hard in preparing and trying your case, the jury will want to ease the pain of your client's devastating loss. And more often than not, that will mean success.

9/11 and the Victim Compensation Fund

They were always there, but I never really saw them. The Woolworth Building with its wedding cake–white terra cotta was a masterpiece. The Statue of Liberty and its shimmering beacon standing alone and strong made me proud. The Brooklyn Bridge with its elegant spiderweb of cables and powerful towers of peaceful granite was soothing. These were the beauties, the classics. These I would notice, look for, point out to the out-of-towners.

But the Twin Towers were huge, that's all. Only on rainy, dreary days did I glance. Then the tops would disappear in the clouds like two rigid modern-day beanstalks stretching into the heavens.

The downtown Manhattan skyline and its glittering buildings were the backdrop to my life. In the gritty Brooklyn neighborhood where I was raised, the F train was the umbilical cord to the city. You board in the subterranean grime only to escape the darkness a few stops later as it climbs an elevated trestle into the light with the most magnificent views of lower Manhattan, a distant, almost alien, world of wealth and power.

Throughout my life, this downtown skyline of shiny skyscrapers remained a constant. They were there when I jogged along the shore, drove the ugly and decrepit Gowanus Expressway, traveled to and from work in midtown. I passed the giant sleek Towers daily—

ordinary in the day, yet dramatic at night with a patchwork of lights silhouetting the sky.

And then, on a bright, cheerful September morn, they were gone, reduced to a pile of twisted steel and broken hearts. Fire and smoke rising from hell just like the good nuns had warned. Amid the debris and rising with the stream of black ash that lazily drifted over my home were the souls of so many fine young Americans.

I had a deposition that Tuesday, so I was in my midtown office early to prepare. Ordinarily, I would have exited the Brooklyn Battery Tunnel a block or so from the Towers at the time the first plane struck. But the merciful yet demanding God did not spare all. By the time I returned home that afternoon, the list of those lost was long and sad. The quiet of that clear night was broken by the keening of the tormented family in the home behind ours. These tears joined ours as we silently prayed for Jimmy Quinn, my 23-year-old cousin, who worked, as he often said, "on top of the world"—the 101st floor of Tower 1.

The phone rang and names were whispered—Little Jimmy Riches, Captain Vinny Brunton, two of the Langs, Dennis O'Berg's kid, Megan O'Grady's husband . . . . And neighbors, one up the block, one down, firefighters, traders, those with rotten luck. In my tribal Brooklyn world where the fire department and Wall Street were not simply jobs but sacred vocations, the list never seemed to end. Xaverian, the local Catholic high school, attended by my brothers and son, lost 23 graduates. My 16-year-old daughter Lizzy's classmate was on the front page of *The News* attending her father's funeral. "And did you know the Lynch brothers . . . you know the cop who went back inside, Moira Smith, she grew up on 74th Street . . . remember Charlie Kasper, you played against him in the schoolyard"—all too familiar. All too painful.

At first, the days were consumed with passionate prayers for miracles. They were fueled by hope that, some way, Jimmy and his innocent smile would stroll out of the pit and have another story to add to his endless list. Then the days slowed, the hope faded, the faith wavered. And, faced with the searching eyes of children, there were no soothing answers. As Yeats wrote, "All changed, changed utterly . . . ."

During these early days, with photos of the missing plastered throughout the city, Congress, on September 22, 2001, passed a bailout bill for the airlines and, almost forgetting the victims, hastily added the September 11th Victim Compensation Fund (VCF) of 2001. This no-fault alternative to litigation would provide compensation through an administrative procedure for those injured or killed. In exchange, the act barred lawsuits against all but the terrorists and their organizations. The hastily written law provided little detail or explanation. It allowed, however, an award to include both economic and non-economic loss. How these elements were to be calculated was unclear. The VCF was to be administered by a Special Master appointed by then-Attorney General John Ashcroft.

Since our firm specializes in plaintiff wrongful death cases from airline and other disasters, and because we represented many families of Pan Am 103, a 1988 terrorist attack, we were contacted to provide guidance, to interpret the language of "eligible individual," "collateral source," "economic loss," "non-economic loss." Would it be fair, who can apply, how will it work? Should I sue or enter the Fund? Scared, angry, battered by grief were the widows, parents, siblings. Since this legislation was without precedent, any answer was mere conjecture.

Bob Clifford of Chicago and I were asked to brief the Department of Justice on issues that would arise from the plaintiffs' viewpoint. They were myriad. Who is entitled to recover? What is an injury? How would damages be calculated? How would they be distributed? What would constitute a collateral source offset? Would the results mirror the tort system? What documentation would be required? What about stock options, discount rate, consumption, workers' compensation, the incalculable suffering that forced between 50 and 200 to jump? What about those living together but not married? Same-sex couples? Those single without dependents? And on and on and on.

The vague legislation raised more questions than answers. Yet, to succeed, the Fund would have to convince nearly 3,000 skeptical families to enter the program, primarily based on faith in the goodness and integrity of their government, a faith shattered that bright, clear morn.

The September 11 families were mostly young, educated, and wonderful. They all had relatives, friends who were money managers, lawyers, doctors, accountants. The frantic phone calls from the inferno of suffocating smoke and buckling floors were a window into their generosity, their overwhelming love of family.

Trapped with no hope, one victim calmly told his wife he loved her very much and then informed her where the life insurance policies were, the stock option plan. "I'm not getting out. Tell the kids I love them all very much." Then the phone disconnected. Another, speaking to a relative through a wet towel: "I'm not getting out of here. Will you please help care for Sue (due to give birth that week) and the children?"

There were no words of self-pity. In often trembling voices, their only thoughts were of their wives and their precious little ones they had seen for the last time.

Those in Tower 2 reassured their loved ones that they were fine: The plane hit the other Tower. After all, they were told to stay by the building management of Tower 2: "Everything's fine, return to your desks." Shaken, they described the raging fire, the white paper that so often defines our work eerily floating by, and the many leaping from heat and horror into eternity. In all those poignant conversations, the word *love* is the linchpin.

Whether running bravely into the Towers or desperately trying to escape, those whose earthly remains disappeared that day were successful in every sense. Family-oriented, loving spouses, magnificent as mothers and fathers. They attended church, coached T-ball and soccer, worked and played hard surrounded by large and loving family and friends. I've handled hundreds of death cases, most very good and fine people, but no group can compare to the September 11 victims.

Most death is tragedy. But the devastation of 9/11 was not in the collapse of the solid concrete and steel symbols of our success, but in the theft of such promise and goodness of so many talented young people. For it was the young who died that cloudless day. And the ripples of anguish spread through wealthy suburbs, the outer boroughs, where the young laugh and play. The tears flowed freely in Manhasset and Bay Ridge, Hoboken and Staten Island. Most were young husbands and fathers—near perfect at both. Widows, robbed of secure, happy lives, still had to change diapers, pay bills, and drive their kids to school. They were compelled to appear strong, waiting until their children's nightmares ceased before crying silently in the dark. I spoke to groups on Long Island, in Jersey or New Canaan, to cautious, vulnerable, intelligent, determined families who bonded in their misery.

This Fund was unprecedented, and Congress provided little guidance. With mortgages and tuitions to pay, finances were a concern. So the questions flew—my husband made a lot of money, will there be a cap? Traders at Cantor Fitzgerald, Keefe Bruyette, or Sandler O'Neill made boatloads of money. How will future income be determined in professions where salary is minimal but commissions monumental? What about pay that varies from year to year? How will the intangibles—taking out the garbage, mowing the lawn, putting a bandage on a boo-boo—be valued?

"We're old and my son lived downstairs. He took us shopping, drove us to the doctors. We relied on him for everything. Who's going to help us now?"

"My husband would have retired from the Fire Department next year at half pay and had plans to work his carpentry business full-time. Will that be considered?"

The questions flew—who's entitled to recover? What damage law applies? How will the monies be divided? And who would decide—the VCF or the probate court? What happens with an infant's portion? Who manages, oversees those funds?

It was an impossible task to satisfy everyone—or anyone. And with information then beginning to trickle out about how porous our borders were, and how asleep our government was, the families felt betrayed, and the only visible government face was the VCF.

On November 26, 2001, Attorney General Ashcroft nominated Ken Feinberg as Special Master to run the Fund, determine awards, make the dead rise and the tears stop. With a background as a mediator of renown and former chief of staff of Senator Ted Kennedy's office, Feinberg seemed like a smart, but somewhat unusual, selection by the attorney general.

A man of sometimes unbelievable energy, Feinberg plunged right in, meeting families, addressing groups, encouraging applications, trying to soothe the worried. But the task was monumental and strewn with land mines. As soon as he answered a group on Long Island, everyone from Massachusetts to England knew. The Internet was the tool, and the families became proficient at organizing and communicating. And like any system, inequities arose. Why should my life insurance payment be a setoff when my husband used our after-tax dollars to plan for his death? The families that had life insurance are penalized, but those without life insurance are not. If my award is $2 million and I have $1 million in life insurance, I receive $1 million. But someone in the same situation without life insurance will receive the full $2 million. How is that fair?

I gave birth to my son, raised him, loved him for 31 years. His wife knew him for three years, married nine months. Am I not entitled to anything? I don't even have a say in where he's buried.

We were engaged, the date for our marriage was set, we lived together. I'm not even considered?

I don't want money. I want answers. Why didn't the government stop this Bin Laden? Clinton, Bush knew about him for years and did nothing. Why did security at Logan just waive them through? Why was my husband told by the Port Authority to remain at his desk in Tower 2 when the Port Authority, which runs Newark airport, knew other planes were hijacked and in the air? Why didn't those FDNY radios work in the Towers? They didn't function in the first attack in 1993 and still weren't fixed! Why were the Towers exempted from the NYC Building Code? If they had more stairwells, all those trapped, estimated at 1,500, may have survived.

Like every mass-disaster litigation, each family's situation is unique. But at least in litigation we know most of the rules, the law, and the precedent so we can provide advice based on experience. Here, there were no rules, no precedent, and this wasn't an accident but the worst attack on America in history. And we had been repeatedly warned that it would occur.

As a mediator, Ken Feinberg had worked with lawyers who knew that the negotiating process was part blarney; facts and deadlines could slip and slide so long as there was an outcome. The families, however, wanted definitive answers. So if he said he would look into an issue and respond in two weeks, the families were waiting 14 days later. If there was no response then, the families remembered and distrust grew. Within their therapy groups or family advocacy organizations, they were organized and committed.

The VCF was a monetary system. Yet money was not paramount for almost all 9/11 families. Instead, they sought fairness, honesty, and compassion from a government, which, as we now know, failed them. They were good people, most from modest backgrounds, and did not need or want more than what they deserved. They knew that their spouses, children, siblings died solely because they went to work. They did not want that work demeaned, or the decedent's memory minimized. They expected respect and demanded that it be given, for they had lost all. They needed an acknowledgment of worth.

I know the value of death actions, having handled hundreds over the years. These were monumental: 40-year-old trader averaging $3 million W-2 income for the past five years, two small children; or 38, earning $900,000 with three small kids; or 31, married, earning $225,000. And these weren't unusual. There were hundreds of such individuals—rising at 5 A.M., working under intense pressure all day, and then entertaining clients at night. Most were from working-class backgrounds who only knew work and all the time, then came home to bright, beautiful families.

Through his travels Ken Feinberg began to acquire a sense of the monumental problem. Always upbeat, he radiated optimism in the most pessimistic time. Initially, he was a bit brusque, concerned, but not sensitive to the anguish. He gave lawyer responses to emotional questions. As a result, distrust grew. Families refused to accept his word. So he published interim rules on December 21, 2001, delineating who could make claims and how much they could collect, as well as outlining the method by which claims would be made and awards granted.

For someone to be eligible to receive compensation for personal injuries, the person must have suffered "physical harm" while "present at" the World Trade Center or the Pentagon or in the "immediate aftermath." Only those who suffered physical injury and sought medical treatment within 24 hours (later expanded to 72 hours in the Final Rules) would be entitled to recover. This standard is much more restrictive than ordinary personal injury common-law standards.

In addition to these regulations, the Special Master published presumptive loss-calculation tables, but these tables only calculated loss for income levels up to the 98th percentile of individual income in the United States, or $231,000. For example, probably one-third of the 658 Cantor Fitzgerald employees who were killed earned more than $231,000. The families believed that this constituted a maximum award since Feinberg said that awards above this percentile would "rarely be necessary to ensure that the financial needs of a claimant are met." Many felt that those who earned the most would be penalized in the Fund. This belief compounded the agony, since the Towers were targeted, they knew, because they symbolized our financial success.

From the work/life-expectancy table—for a 25-year-old, the expected retirement age was 59—to the growth rate of the victim's earnings—9.744 percent for a 25-year-old down to 3 percent for a victim over the age of 52, the families found the interim rules restrictive and unjust. The rules did not take into account the profiles of those who died, many of whom worked as traders or firefighters or police officers. The rules were geared toward those who work for salaries with incremental raises each year. Here, you had a 41-year-old single mother making $1 million one year and $350,000 the next, or a 42-year-old fire lieutenant earning $60,000 but working a second job as a bartender earning half as much in cash. After 20 years, this cop or firefighter could retire at half pay tax-free for life and then start another career. The traditional economic model formulated by the Fund and used in most wrongful death actions was not applicable to many who were murdered that summer day.

With these rules, Ken Feinberg put his foot in the water and quickly withdrew it: The reception was icy. Yet he kept meeting, explaining that he would consider a child's learning disability, a decedent who had just made partner, the accounting, carpentry, yard work that will now have to be paid for.

Despite significant comment and criticism, the Final Rules were released on March 13, 2002, with provisions only slightly more generous than the Interim Rules. Feinberg was hesitant to alter the traditional economic model. Instead, he promised that all of these differing circumstances would be considered before he issued an award. Yet criticisms continued, especially in the non-economic area where a flat $250,000 was awarded for the victim's non-economic loss and a meager $100,000 for each child. This was particularly disturbing since so many of the children were infants, and the present value of Social Security payments was a collateral offset. So, if a victim had a healthy 17-year-old daughter, the non-economic award was $100,000 less a few thousand that this young woman would be paid by Social Security. If the victim left a one-month-old with health issues, the family would still receive only $100,000, but the Social Security deduction would be more than $125,000. Many objected that the families who need the most assistance, those with more and younger children, were being shortchanged.

With so many unresolved and what were initially perceived as unfair issues, families were unsure of what to do. They went through a series of emotions, from despair to anger to sadness. Some became activists; others formed therapy groups and bonded with other widows. Most struggled to get out of bed each morning, to dress and feed the children, to smile occasionally, and to lie when asked how they were doing. Luckily, most had extended families that were there to assist. But no one, except each other, truly understood.

So the families moved slowly. They interviewed two or three law firms before they retained an attorney. They knew that bar associations provided pro bono representation, but found that some of those lawyers were inexperienced in death cases and preferred to hire a specialist. Very few accepted the Fund without reservation and entered immediately. They had time to decide and they did not want to waive their right to sue without proof that they would be treated properly. Ironically, those who died were deeply patriotic, but this tragedy made their families question their government.

During this process, we attorneys met with Feinberg, constantly urging him to be flexible with the rules, with what he considered computing an award. My clients were sophisticated and knew what they would recover in a tort action. They wanted to meet Feinberg, explain the loss, the devastation, the effect on their children. Litigation, I often explain, will only provide compensation. It will never achieve what you want—having your smiling son walk through the door carrying a pizza.

Since the VCF application was Joe Friday–like, "Just the facts," we decided to supplement the filing with a brochure that portrayed the decedent not only in economic terms but, what is really important in life, as a person, a husband, daughter, brother, friend. So we compiled photos, obtained written statements from friends, relatives, and co-workers describing the individual, his attributes, and the impact of the loss on the family. We garnered medical, psychiatric, and employment records. An expert economist projected financial loss. We acquired the children's school and medical records. We copied the tender notes from the softball team that named their field after their beloved coach.

Parents, spouses, and siblings wrote moving, adoring testimonials—how they miss the brilliant smile and boisterous laugh, the bear hugs and silly nicknames, the Sunday morning optimism which inevitably turned to familiar despair as the Jets blew another one, the wild parties, the quiet strolls along the shore, and the teaching of the Hail Mary to his sleepy-eyed beauty in her sunflower pj's.

These brochures provided not only a description of economic loss but also the loss of love and guidance, the end of carefree Saturday nights of beer and burgers, of the comforting reassurance that Sally's fever of 103 will eventually end. They told stories of ordinary people living unique and special lives. Not all saints, of course, but fine people doing mostly good.

After much work and many revisions, these brochures contained the essence of the decedent and his family, from the hilarious photos with his college roomies to the family portrait that sits on the piano. Even though we created these, the indecision was such that the families still did not want to submit applications. They wanted reassurance that the Fund would not shortchange them. Even though Feinberg promised fairness, they did not know what that meant. With myriad troublesome questions and issues, he had on occasion contradicted himself, so the families wanted proof that he would consider the intangibles, since the written rules were, in their view, harsh and niggardly. Deciding whether to sue or enter the Fund was difficult for a bunch of reasons. So everyone waited.

One of my high school friends lost his wife. He had married late and had no children, so he decided to enter the Fund. Adverse to any thought of litigation, he believed that the Fund was best for him both emotionally and financially. This became the test case. So we created a brochure and submitted an unsigned application with all pertinent documentation. After the material was evaluated by the Fund, we arranged for a hearing in March 2003 before Feinberg where my client testified under oath. Since there was no signed application, this hearing was technically informal.

Feinberg gave a brief description of the decedent and then summarized her economic loss based on the tax returns and information submitted, highlighting any area that he wanted amplified. He then detailed the collateral offsets—insurance payments, pension, and the $255 Social Security death payment. I opened with a short introduction, summarizing the couple and their dreams, how they had just purchased a co-op in Bay Ridge, and how she was in the process of furnishing it when she was killed. Tragically, though she worked uptown, she was giving a presentation in Tower 1 when the attack occurred.

My client then spoke of his love, his loss, his pain. Graciously, he acknowledged how impossible the role of Special Master was, how difficult it was to evaluate a life in monetary terms, and even apologized for a particularly contentious session in Staten Island where Feinberg was met with derision and rage. Lasting about 45 minutes, the hearing was successful. My client voiced his suffering, explained some economic issues that the rules did not address adequately, and listened to the Special Master agonize over the many complex issues compounded by emotion. At the end, Feinberg gave a net minimum award after collateral offsets, which was satisfactory to me and my client. And fair.

Pleased that the hearing went well, we signed the application and a few months later received an award letter with a bit more than was promised at the hearing. This confirmed what I had thought—Feinberg's word was good. I spread the news among my clients who still remained cautious. Our test case was relatively straightforward. No children, years of earnings history within the 98 percentile, well-documented benefits. But what was significant was not the calculation, but that Feinberg listened, understood, and was relatively flexible.

But this did not encourage many others to enter. Instead, they agreed to submit an unsigned application with a brochure. Provide all the information, meet with him, and listen to his proposed minimum award. Then they could decide to enter. And gradually a few came forward, met with the Special Master, spoke their souls, listened, and answered his questions. Still many could not take the final step of filing the executed application. Of course, we told our clients that litigation against the airlines and others was not certain success. Even though we believed we could win such a battle, it would take longer and be more costly, and there was no guarantee that the recovery would be substantially greater.

Every month or so, another survivor provided documents, attended a hearing, and expressed her agony, her fear, how September 11 transformed a happy, successful family into misery and illness. Feinberg would listen, express compassion, marvel at the courage and the resiliency of the children. Those who met with him proceeded to submit executed applications, receive award letters, and be satisfied with the process. We met with him in New York, Boston, and Washington—for the fanaticism of the terrorists knew no limits of age, religion, or geography.

Yet Feinberg realized that without a firm deadline, many would never decide. Paralyzed by fear, grief, indecision, whatever, they delayed. December 22, 2003, was the date all applications had to be in. And at the last moment, hundreds were filed. I encouraged all my 125 clients to send in their applications because I knew they would be treated equitably. I also recommended hearings primarily with Feinberg himself or his intelligent, sensitive Assistant Special Master, Debby Greenspan.

Obviously, this was not possible. So, after a flood of applications was submitted at the last minute, volunteer attorneys conducted the sworn hearings. PricewaterhouseCoopers accumulated and digested the economic data. We were in constant contact with them, talking many times each day, responding to requests for pension, income information, original death certificates, providing medical documentation of little Charlie's juvenile diabetes. The process became streamlined as trust grew and procedures became known.

Of course, not all those affected by the attacks died. One miracle of that morning is the number who escaped both Towers before the collapses. The seriously physically injured and those rescue workers who developed respiratory problems during the cleanup also submitted claims. The stories of being trapped, burned, looking for an exit, knowing others could not escape, although well publicized, were distressing and haunting when that person was sitting next to you. Because there were so few seriously injured individuals and injuries—burns over 30 percent of your body—are more difficult to quantify, these cases presented problems for the Special Master.

In these injury cases, we provided photos, extensive physician affidavits detailing the diagnosis and prognosis, schedules of surgical procedures and brief, yet descriptive, summaries of each. We even videotaped a treating surgeon's statement to help the Fund understand the magnitude of treatment. This was effective, but not as much as the sight of the scars, the Jobs bandage, the client's recitation of jet fuel cascading into the elevator.

Feinberg dealt with them with sensitivity. He was particularly understanding to those in the parochial world of the FDNY who lost so many. Three of my firefighter families lost sons who had followed their fathers into this service, one leaving a CPA career to run into burning buildings that everyone else was fleeing. One father, a battalion chief with three firefighter sons, barely survived both collapses. The other two fathers spent months at the site, vainly hoping to save someone, not leaving until the site was clear, until the battered, yet empty bunker gear with the yellow lettering of the names were all found. Only then could a funeral be held with the crushed helmet placed on the casket before the altar.

Like so many, Feinberg had trouble understanding the allure, the camaraderie of the FDNY. Actually, it's a modern-day religious order with its hierarchy, uniforms, financial security, but more importantly, friendship, courage, and service to others. The attraction is such that a few fire officers, who retired on disability after 9/11, sued to return to the job even though they would earn less. They would prefer to work in a dangerous job for less money than stay home and watch the Mets lose again.

So, except for one client with unusual circumstances, all our clients entered the Fund. We rushed to complete the brochures, respond to PricewaterhouseCoopers, and hold hearings. And we did. The hearings became procedurally routine but heart-wrenching each time. And Feinberg worked like a maniac. If we needed to be in front of him, we would schedule 10 or so hearings in a day, starting at 9 A.M., each lasting a half hour since there was never enough time. The tears flowed, the anguish was revealed, the anxiety was confessed. He would listen, tilt his head back and try to reassure, tell them he would consider the handicapped child, the devastated mother, the loss of security, the loss of guidance. They needed to bare their emotions, talk about the perfect daughter, and "how Jim used to make me laugh. And I don't laugh anymore, Mr. Feinberg."

So we struggled through the hearings, received awards, disbursed the money, and tried to ensure that it was invested properly. Rarely were there disputes, since most had intact families. Problems did occur, usually in fractured families and, on occasion, between a widow and her in-laws, especially if there were no children. These battles were transferred to probate court where they usually settled, but not without tension and ugly accusations.

In the end, the generous American people paid a total of almost $7 billion. The 2,878 death awards of the 2,973 who died averaged $2.1 million and ranged from $250,000 to $7.1 million. Some 2,675 injury awards were granted, primarily to rescue workers, and another 1,800 were denied. These awards ranged from $500 to $8.7 million. Approximately 100 families whose relatives died opted for traditional litigation, primarily those who were passengers on the planes. The Fund closed June 15, 2004, and those involved returned to their routines.

For most, of course, the Victim Compensation Fund was a minor part of this terrible horror—a horror repeated in Madrid and London and, most likely, again in New York. But the Fund did not exacerbate the suffering and may have helped ever so slightly in healing. And when I walk the gum-stained sidewalks of Bay Ridge, I'm on streets named in honor of those who left for work and never returned—Mark D. Hindy, Constantine "Gus" Economos, Moira Smith, Pamela C. Boyce, Billy Lake, Kathleen Hunt Casey. The saloons advertise the golf outings, the 5K races, the charity events in the memories of these who were once young. But on those same streets children play and laugh and grow. Yet peace comes dropping slow for all the rest.

Part Three

A Trial Lawyer's Life

Before and Now

I began practicing law as the sun popped over the horizon, chasing the dark and warming the tranquil bay. Before the late 1970s, law was a fraternity on an orange-bright autumn afternoon, with boys in striped ties strolling across a lush green to a noisy stadium, carelessly smiling at the wonder of their world. Oh sure, some guys with sharp elbows and minds from Flatbush or Woodside climbed out of the subway downtown and entered those polished rooms where deals were negotiated with a few polite words, a nod, and a firm handshake. The hurricane of the 1960s and early 1970s rattled this serene corner of America, but strong oak doors and tightly woven oriental rugs kept the rabble outside.

A profession, that's what it was way back when. Battles occurred, but in soft, crooning voices and respectful tones. Contracts, briefs, and motions were typed by proper, efficient women from the Grace Institute. Letters were dictated in confident words from three-piece gray suits. Carbon paper blackened your hands and occasionally your white shirt. Pockets were stuffed with dimes so a call from court could detail the judge's decision. It was "Mad Men" practice law.

It now seems like the Dark Ages. When cute, nervous secretaries skipped a word or phrase, the result was audible sighs and groans, for the page had to be retyped. Everything took time, from dialing the phone to Shepardizing cases to opening the mail. Typewriter repairmen made monthly visits, mailmen strained to carry bundles, harried receptionists scribbled telephone messages. An era of Wite-Out and special erasable paper, of cut-and-paste editing, of hand-delivered letters, of desks piled high with volumes of New York Supplements, where a skilled secretary was more valued than a senior partner.

Then came gradual change—copy machines proliferated, IBM Selectrics allowed typos to be corrected by backspacing, dictating equipment with giant microphones and tape replaced shorthand, telexes magically sent brief messages overseas. There were rudimentary computers and fax machines with paper that faded after a few months.

Change accelerated. As I was watching my kids turn into annoying teenagers, the Net, voicemail, laptops, cell phones materialized. Books, newspapers, entire law libraries disappeared, and you'll serve hard time if you ever try to file a single paper in federal court where e-filing is mandatory. And now there's Google and iPhones and Facebook and Twitter and blogs. Everyone knows everything about you, and we've all seen photos of you doing tequila shots.

It isn't only technology that has changed in the 30-plus years since I anxiously entered the old Pan Am building the morning after Labor Day for my first day as a lawyer. In law school, I interned for Maxine Duberstein and Sybil Hart Kooper, the first female Supreme Court justices in Kings County (only in New York is the Supreme Court the trial court). Older women would enter the courtroom, sit quietly until a break, and then approach and tell those judges, whom they didn't know, how proud they were.

Lawsuits and deals multiplied, new judges appeared daily, firms hired until there were hundreds, thousands of lawyers. The weak vanished, and the strong demanded more—lawyers, clients, money. And we know that at some time (probably when we were talking to the architect about the new room off the kitchen) the profession that I joined became a business and—poof!—gone were the days of loyalty and friendship and care (if they ever existed).

But my purpose is not to lament a world of which I had little part. My education was on uneven, cracked sidewalks with only the occasional strong London plane tree providing shade from the smelly heat.

Like many, I profited from the tsunami of litigation, especially personal injury cases, the headline-grabbing jury verdicts, the medmal suits, the product liability lawsuits, and the innovative arguments which led to successful recoveries. Whether these myriad changes, including a more callous law firm attitude toward partners—"Hey, we love you, but you're not generating sufficient business. Your last day is December 31st."—were good or bad, I'll leave to those more thoughtful to determine.

I love Google and YouTube and Facebook and blogs, the photos of my relatives' kids adorable in their March shamrocks or in party dresses all grown up. I can friend guys I haven't seen for decades and see photos of their long-gone parents, of blessed memory. I can check the Yankees' score after each batter; no more running to the candy store to buy *The News*, praying that Duke Snider hit a homer or the Newk pitched a shutout. I love the ease, the access to the world's knowledge, and I'm happy that carbon paper no longer sullies my pale skin.

Yet when I hold a newspaper in my hands—yes, I'm that antiquated—I inevitably learn about the darker side: sexting, dialing drunk, cyberstalking, and I wonder whether it's a net plus overall. In the movie *Up in the Air,* the oh-so-capable young woman follows a boy to Omaha only to be dumped via text message. "Texting is the devil. Stop it," advises Professor Kerry Cronin of Boston College, who mandates that her students go on a date in order to pass her class. Funny, right? Until she relates that one student asked:

"But where would we go?"
"I don't know, but there's this city called Boston."
"And how would we get there?"
"The T [mass transit], just a guess."
"But then we'd have to talk all the time we're on the T."
"Yes, that's a date," the good professor exclaims. (See Professor Cronin's "Rules of the 1st Date" on YouTube.)

Professor Cronin laments the hook-up generation where oral communication is non-existent, all words are electronic. Where my daughter phones from her room in our house (maybe 50 feet away) to tell me to shut up when I'm screaming like a maniac after an Eli

Manning touchdown. Where students in law school classes rarely look up from their computer screens. Where one third-year law student, a professor noted, was watching graphic porn during class. Alas, all we ever had was the tabloids.

We know that kids spend too much time on cells, computers, and video games. Hey, our parents thought we'd amount to nothing because we watched too much television. And, maybe they were right. But I won't lecture to shut off the iPhone, sit in Starbucks and discuss world politics. It's useless, like commanding the tide to stay out. Instead, I hope for some common sense by those raised by Steve Jobs and Sergey Brin, who have 876 friends on Facebook and who sent 1,246 texts last month.

Is it a requirement that every under-30-year-old has at least one photo with both middle fingers raised? Or sake bombing, like my then-underage daughter? A 40-something sitting on the toilet is not funny. Even my juvenile sense of humor says "Enough." If you don't want grandma to see it, don't post it. Law schools, employers check Facebook and other social media sites in evaluating applicants. What is hilarious when you're 21 may be viewed as repulsive to someone 51.

Some post a picture of every meal. It's a way to "share their lives," or stick to a diet, according to *The New York Times.* I'm not that interested in what I eat, never mind your bowl of Frosted Flakes. And I already know you're fat.

Professional athletes and others e-mail photos of their private parts to women who immediately post them on the Net. They're not just vulgar now; these images will be seen by their teenage children someday. Photos are like cockroaches. They can't ever be eradicated.

Your personal life is, well, personal. So you enjoyed your breakfast fish fry with a cold Leinenkugel. You thought the silent movie *The Artist* was quaint. You're reading *The Seven Habits of Highly Effective People.* Fine. But I don't care if you've finally met your soulmate, had a spat with your girlfriend, or have a runny nose. Really, other than the people you live with, no one does.

Ballerinas tweet during intermission, detailing bumps, bruises, and, please God, don't let me be fat. NBA players have been fined for tweeting during a game. Celebrities complain about having no personal life but then tweet that they just had a latte or that they're separating from their one true love. Even Miley Cyrus said that she stopped posting information on Twitter because she can't complain about lack of privacy and then tweet that she took a shower.

I don't get it. Why does everyone want the world to know everything? I'm not that interesting—and neither are you. You're a lawyer, not a rock star. You write briefs that, at best, are clear. Fitzgerald or Hemingway, you aren't. In your heels and simple jewelry, you litigate disputes concerning money.

Wedding sites abound, detailing the first date, and first kiss, with photos of the groom-to-be on bended knee. I guess it was similar when I was in college and some pretty would march into the silent library, thrust out her finger, and scream, "I got engaged." Now the brash announcement is electronic, with far too much minutiae on the relationship, the church, the reception, and the honeymoon. It's part of the "Look at Me" phenomenon, the "I'm the First Ever to Get Married," the "I'm the First Ever to Have a Baby" syndrome.

It's easy to send an e-mail belittling work or effort, dump someone via text, or repeat cruel gossip. It's much more difficult to call, say these words, and listen to a reaction. And it is impossible for most to sit and state them face-to-face. Impersonal communication allows cowards to transmit nasty, malicious words without repercussion or response. The sad suicides of teens may be caused, in part, by cyberbullying. If you can't say it to someone's face, don't e-mail or text it.

Do more talking. In person. Sure it's more work than e-mail, but so much more rewarding. Stop checking your phone every second and have a sustained conversation. That's how you actually know a person.

Stop multitasking. Driving while texting, e-mailing while talking, browsing while on conference calls ("Guilty, Your Honor"). An MIT study proved that we don't really multitask. We just switch attention from one task to another, extremely quickly, spending less and less time on each of many more topics. You can only focus on one at a time. It's hard to concentrate, easy to flit about without reverie or much thought. Be a bit more European; sip a glass of wine and talk, linger over the dinner table. Sit on a park bench and watch the parade. And then tell someone about it.

On occasion, step away from technology. A Georgia Tech basketball team gave up cell phones for the ACC and NCAA tournaments. One player mentioned that every two seconds someone had been hitting them up, texting or calling. Without them, the team focused, talked more. Not enough to win, but there's no doubt that constantly responding to texts and e-mails hinders serious and deep reflection and concentration.

I often wonder how we functioned those many years ago when I was a naïve new lawyer. But long before that, our ancestors built the Coliseum, the Pyramids, even the Brooklyn Bridge. It took longer, was more arduous, but people thrived and great works were created. It's quicker and easier today. But better?

Words

While in college nearly 40 years ago, I worked for the guys (that's right, no women) who wrote the editorials at *The New York Times*. I started as a copyboy. My job was to take copy from one editor to another and then to the composing room, where union mugs would retype it on medieval machines, turning the typewritten words into lead from which numerous galleys were printed. I would then hurry those galleys back to the editors, to Mr. Barzilay, who was in charge of the page as it went to bed at night, and to the proofreaders, who had neat, tiny desks on which sharpened pencils sat.

In an hour or two, I would return to the third floor and gather those galleys from the proofreaders, who were older, mostly men in white shirts and simple ties. Inevitably, the galleys were filled with corrections of typos, style, tense, and punctuation. And in meticulous handwriting, questions were posed about the meaning of words or sentences; alternative phrases were suggested.

I worked at *The Times* not because I wanted to be a reporter or anything like that, but because I needed money for jeans, rock concerts, and gas for my tan Volkswagen Bug. Back then, my generation knew it all. We would eradicate poverty, end racism, and spread peace and love over the globe. So I viewed the proofreaders with a certain disdain and pity, since I couldn't imagine a more boring, unproductive job.

Mostly, I worked weekends, when the pace was slower and I had time to do homework or thumb through the paper or a magazine. I even started to read the editorial galleys and would try to identify typos, fix punctuation. Since I had attended Holy Name Grammar School, where we spent endless days diagramming sentences, memorizing the difference between a participle and a gerund, and participating in continuous spelling bees, I thought I was pretty good. Yet I was nowhere close to the precision and accuracy of the proofreaders.

If we were on deadline, my job would be to find the proofreader working on our editorials and gently tell him to hurry up. I would stand near the main desk until he came scurrying. Since it was a solitary job, the proofreaders would often explain corrections, discuss questions regarding the meaning of a word, and didn't I think this phrase was more exact? All this was said with muted enthusiasm and a touch of awe.

I was always taught that work was, well, work. You weren't supposed to like it. Just do it; stop complaining. But this group, who did work that looked boring to me, really seemed to enjoy their jobs. It soon became obvious that it wasn't really the work they loved but words. All words.

Gradually, my opinion of the proofreaders began to change. Sure, it was still the era of "Don't trust anyone over 30" and all that, but even I matured a bit and began to understand the remarkable devotion and passion these people had for words and their use. And, much to my surprise, I slowly grasped the beauty and majesty of words.

My awareness of the power of words grew as I worked for the editorial department and witnessed the steady stream of politicians coming as supplicants to the 10th floor of *The Times* building off then-seedy Times Square. It would be storybook to add that this is why I became a lawyer, the natural progression of language from newspaper to courtroom. Well, not really. I became a lawyer essentially by accident, but my work and learning at *The Times* has probably been of more benefit than all my schooling combined.

So, those many years ago, I realized not only the significance of words but their power and beauty. And words, of course, are what we as lawyers mostly use. We are advocates, dispensing wisdom and guidance through language, writing briefs, arguing motions, cross-examining witnesses, researching law. We are inundated with words—both comforting and threatening. With the Net and technology, communication is instantaneous and omnipresent, popping up on iPhones at the beach or golf course. It's a far cry from the typewriters, Wite Out, and carbon paper that were the norm when I began practicing.

Yet this mostly wonderful technology has had a great impact on words, their meaning, spelling (just read any of my daughters' e-mails), and especially their power, given the ease of immediate worldwide dissemination. In the past, to read and copy a court document, you had to run to the courthouse, request the file, and hope the copier machine wasn't broken. Today you can do it all from your office and forward it to innumerable recipients with a push of a button. The world can almost immediately read or hear or view whatever is written or said either in our profession or among those who are in the public domain.

Of course, many (including me) will argue that it is not technology alone which has changed language, but also our value system itself: the failure to teach writing in our schools, the emphasis of the visual over the written, and the "dumbing down" of our culture, as Senator Pat Moynihan preached. Behavior once thought abhorrent is now accepted as normal. Words that were curses when I was young—suck, pissed, bastard, bitch—are now vernacular. Words of ridicule that were rarely used because their meaning was so telling, so powerful, and so devastating are thrown about without thought or consideration—whore, slut, racist, moron. Words that ridicule racial, ethnic, or religious groups are fodder for wannabe shock jocks.

Even in our legal practice, a heated telephone conversation used to remain private, with no transcript of the regrettable anger. With e-mail, the invective, said on a bad day at a bad time, cannot be eradicated and can be sent to many, prolonging and increasing the vitriol. So the combination of technology and cultural deterioration has coarsened our profession. Instead of being used for praise and reward, words are used to batter and bludgeon and destroy, like so many movies and video games we allow our children to view.

We have become free and loose with powerful and harmful words, using them for the slightest reason or with no reason at all. Exaggeration has replaced precision. Not only in rap music or on the Bay Ridge street corners where I live, but in our arguments, our briefs, hurling charges of "deliberately ignoring this Court's order," "intentionally hiding documents," "near criminal activity." Sanctions are sought, disqualification of counsel urged. Even in simple discovery disputes, the venom flows. Fees, costs, and your first-born, I demand it all and more. And I plead guilty, guilty, guilty.

So let's not pretend it's only people like hip-hop rappers who sing about bitches, sluts, and n-words who are to blame for the deterioration of language and the hyperbole which has infected our behavior. Lawyers are part of the problem and, quite frankly, more responsible than the Brooklyn kids who walk past my home to Fort Hamilton High School with their tattoos and belly rings, and four-letter words dripping from glossed lips. We are educated, trained, highly paid professionals, yet our words and actions are often no better than ignorant street punks with the music blasting and the gum clacking. A D.C. administrative judge suing a dry cleaners owned by immigrants for $65 million over a pair of missing pants. Or consider the defense offered by an attorney representing a lawyer accused of raping two teens pimped by their mother: "My client made $500,000 a year. He had the wherewithal to pay for any piece of tuckus on the planet. And he paid for that skank?"

The song and splendor of words are gradually fading amid the harsh screeches that saturate our work. The combination of music and language which pervades Joyce and other great writers is no longer evident in almost all of our culture and profession. It is difficult enough in our briefs and letters, often so formal and dense, to display grace or elegance. But, sadly, most no longer even try. Our preference is to attack and wound. Pick up any document on your overloaded desk and you will read "blatant misconduct," "improperly obtained information" "misuse," "clear breach of ethical standards," "intentionally sought to hide . . . ." And I sit, staring out my window on this warm spring day, and wonder how my adversary— a nice enough guy, I once thought—could allow such statements, both false and boorish, to be memorialized on crisp white paper.

Do not underestimate the power of words said or written so easily in this era of such incredible technology. They may be ignored or forgotten but cannot be erased. Sure, it feels good to voice frustration or displeasure, but civility and professionalism must triumph. We must acknowledge the harm that hateful words not only do to our adversary but to ourselves. We must refrain from their use; avoid temptation to muddy our opposition and our reputation. For it is only then that we will realize the splendor of our words.

Hubris

I could never understand how pride could be a sin, even though I was taught it was the worst—worse than murder or stealing or gluttony or lust, whatever that was. Adam and Eve's pride got them tossed out of Eden, which I thought was no big deal since Paradise sounded pretty boring except for the nude part. Eating fruit in some verdant garden under a tree sounded a bit like hell to me. Now, if they had been scarfing down a slice at Mom's pizzeria on Prospect Park West after a few hours of playing basketball in the schoolyard—that, my friends, would have been heaven.

Of course, as I've aged and personally experienced (if not committed) all seven cardinal sins, and not only once, I realize what I learned was accurate. Everyone's a little greedy and the whole country is fat—so, some sins are, well, accepted. Maybe because I now stop and actually look around the shiny, expensive table at a deposition or scan the high-ceilinged, elaborate courtroom, I realize more actions are taken because of ego and conceit than for any other reasons. Insisting on taking the deposition or arguing the motion; hogging the telephone conference; treating associates and staff like crap; refusing to listen; claiming to know everyone and everything; never, ever being wrong. Now, these flaws—usually the products of personal pride—may not land you in Hades for eternity, but they happen all too frequently, demeaning the individual and our profession.

161

I wonder whether there's something in the water at law school that causes such behavior. Otherwise, why the discontent and the need to stand out? After all, we're all pretty bright, or at least good test takers, and compared to the stiff working in a mine in West Virginia or the single mom with two kids living over a bodega in Sunset Park, we're successful. A few are even extremely wealthy— making millions. But it appears that at least for some, that's not enough. What they want is "King of the Hill, A-Number-One, Top of the Heap," as Frankie sang. They'll elbow and scratch and scream and cut corners to get or stay there. As if it matters. As if anyone cares. But obviously, they do. Sometimes I cringe at what I see and read.

Now, I'm no saint. I have a healthy ego except at golf, where I know I stink. Pride has crept up on me from time to time. I have had my share of vulgar incidents that now shame me.

But that's not what I think about. What I prefer to dwell on is the young lawyer who came up to me in court, introduced herself, and said: "You probably don't remember me, but my first deposition ever was in your office. Against you. And I didn't know what I was doing, and you were nice. You could have killed me but you didn't. Thanks."

With that in mind, I try to forget the myriad times my voice was harsh or dripped with sarcasm, causing untold discomfort and aggravation. Most of us have both experiences, but there's no reason for acting like maniacs. It took me time to learn that—too long, in fact.

But what amazes me are not the selfish, offensive actions themselves but how unproductive they are. How they discredit the individual and impair the litigation. By insisting that he should do everything and be Napoleon, the all-knowing lawyer doesn't add to his stature but instead becomes less effective, his reputation diminished, his stature lost. Of course, even such normally boorish actions don't compare with the self-inflicted tragedy of gazillionaires Dickie Scruggs, William Lerach, and Mel Weiss. With more money than all but Warren Buffett and glowing media reviews, these successful lawyers thought they were above it all, so good and powerful that they succumbed to illegalities not for an extra buck but to be the best, *numero uno*. Their pride blinded them, so they no longer lived in the real world. Through arrogance and skill, they believed they could eat the apple and remain in Paradise. It's a shame.

Now, I'm not sure there's a correlation between talking over people at a deposition and thievery. Of course not, right? But there is a common thread, even if boorish conduct rarely becomes criminal. I write this to warn young, and even old, lawyers to resist the temptation to believe you are unique, that you have unparalleled charm and ability. If you do, go find a cure for cancer, which is devastating my family. I was taught early and often that Satan is always present, searching for weakness, ready to pounce. I don't believe all that I learned in those simpler times, but temptation exists and must be fought, even when you know you are the better lawyer and can make a better argument or do a better cross. Remember, such superiority, even if it is true, doesn't give you the right to demean or criticize others or laud your accomplishments over theirs.

Be gracious, even humble. I litigated a case in Lexington, Kentucky, and was amazed at not only the professionalism of these funny, bright southern lawyers, but how they are so understated, polite, and ready to accommodate, all the while being more accomplished than us big-city loudmouths.

So when you hear your voice rise or when you spit sarcastic words, stop and reconsider. Realize that others can also contribute, can also provide insight and intelligence. Hubris often begins with a sense of superiority on ordinary, mundane matters. If you fail to recognize and stop its progression, your arrogance and conceit will not only besmirch your reputation but may potentially ruin your career.

Lies We Tell Ourselves

Paparazzi aren't stalking us as we sip our cappuccino. TMZ will never detail how sexy we look in our Brooks Brothers blue. Certainly, we're not tabloid famous like sad Lindsay Lohan or Charlie Sheen. No trailer with our name sits on a movie set, nor do we stroll the red carpet in Chanel before screaming teens. Sure, I'd love to pal with Jack at Lakers games, have a Sam Adams with Matt Damon in Southie, or split a pasta at Del Posto with Meryl Streep. But I'm not that cool. I'm not Hollywood. Nor are you.

But, still, we *are* in the entertainment business. It's just that we lack the fame, money, and arm candy. We're actors, after all. We stand before a judge or jury and feign outrage, evoke sympathy, and, on occasion, cause a chuckle. When we step into a courtroom, we play a part, a role. We adopt a persona, speak and move with purpose, all to convince a weary, apathetic audience we're right. We memorize lines, argue and beg, strut about, and use many of the skills of Oscar winners in pursuit of success. Alas, no visual effects make us beautiful, nor is there any chance for retakes before someone screams, "That's a wrap!" Our set is real, no 3-D glasses needed. Our performance is spontaneous, done every day all day, and if we bomb, catcalls are heard from clients, partners, spouses, even kids.

Many varied scenes make up our performances, from meeting the client to deposing witnesses to arguing motions to cross-examination. If we're effective and can convince a jury, we win or succeed. But the adulation is brief: We then simply have to do it again, tomorrow, next month, next year. It's a show that never ends: Trial lawyers are thespians, always on stage.

Most lawyers can separate reality from illusion, can drop the facade once the day ends. Others, however, invest such time and effort in the performance that they no longer can separate their thoughts and principles from those of the client. The Kool-Aid is swallowed. Objectivity and perspective vanish.

No longer sage advocates, the just cause becomes their life. Victory becomes proof that integrity and goodness exist, while an unexpected loss is a personal rejection that devastates, leads to self-doubt, anguish, and despair. Here are some of the lies we tell ourselves.

We can't lose. Through this ability to play a role, we convince not only others but sometimes ourselves of the virtue of our arguments. Years of contentious litigation, weeks of trial—hand-to-hand combat, really—too easily leads us to demonize our adversaries and to develop an unquestioning belief in the glorious cause. Every snide remark becomes personal until our emotions trump wisdom. We explain away every adverse ruling and see triumph in every setback, because we refuse to accept the possibility of defeat. We are Ahab chasing the white whale, soldiers fighting to death on Iwo Jima.

And when we start to lose judgment this way, arrogance can invade our personalities and, if we're not careful, our work. Crucial documents are hidden, damaging precedent omitted from briefs, and false accusations are made with gusto. The end, we whisper, justifies the sins committed along the way.

It's easy to become immersed in the minutiae of litigation, the thousands of documents, the ESI issues, the petty disputes that permeate discovery. It's natural to dislike and then despise your adversary: Even routine matters can deteriorate into battles because the stakes are so large and the pressure to succeed so relentless.

Our office and legal environment fosters a parochial perception that your adversary's case is flawed, his abilities modest. Around the conference room table, you and your colleagues mock what you see as the opposition's supercilious attempt to suck up to the judge. You ridicule the plaintiff's devastating injuries and emotional scars as the products of hyperbole and greed. Heads nod and voices applaud the party line. "You'll win . . . don't settle . . . screw those lying . . . ."

Soon this maelstrom of attitudes and self-deception engulfs you, and you're in the eddy, unable to escape. You rebuff settlement. You insult: "I'll never pay a nickel for this piece of crap." You fail to perceive your weaknesses and the vulnerabilities in the facts, the law, yourself. The slam-dunk case becomes a devastating defeat. Now the chorus of sycophants that once urged you to soldier on has quieted and, instead, is now questioning your strategy and judgment.

There are ways to keep yourself from getting into this kind of fix: Before you do something big, or emotional, or attention-getting, consult others, and not those involved in the case. Ask their thoughts before you e-mail the four-page scathing letter over a single deposition objection. Before you scream, "I'll never pay more than . . . ," solicit those you trust, who've been around the block. On nearly every putt, I ask my buddy Joe Taranto for a read. Being stubborn, I only heed his advice half the time, but I always ask. You should, too.

Listen. Yes, we're successful and experienced, but we're not perfect. No, not even you. Get many opinions. Where appropriate, from ordinary folks, too. Take your time. Don't decide based on passion, ego, or conceit.

Use more formalized second opinions, too: jury consultants, mock juries, focus groups. And don't wait until a month before trial. If financially able, hire such people when you are retained, and periodically employ them to shape and enhance your strategy. You'll learn of flaws you never contemplated, problems you didn't believe existed.

It's the other guy's fault. We often justify our sketchy behavior because litigation is war and turning the other cheek is weakness. But remember, you're not in the tribal areas of Pakistan fighting the Taliban. Sure, this case is significant, but it's money, not life or death. We convince ourselves that sharp elbows are essential, cutting corners justified, shady practices permitted because "he did it first." Or "everybody does it." We excuse unethical practices because "we're doing the Lord's work."

I learned very early that each of us has an eternal soul which has understanding and free will. Now, the soul part takes a bit of faith, but I know we can do pretty much whatever we want. We can reject the juvenile tit-for-tat that wastes much of our time. We can practice honorable and aggressive litigation. We can be better. It just takes some decency and guts.

It's not about the money. My philosophy is pure Jerry Maguire: "Show me the money." Others can chant, "It's all about principle, for the good of humanity," and all that bunk. They may even believe it. Yet, for good or bad, almost everything has a price, especially in our profession. Cases settle because it makes smart business sense. Sure, corporations are fleeced, sued unfairly in plaintiff jurisdictions; or, in other places, the horrifically injured receive pennies because jurors are disgusted with reading about the woman who sued the four-year-old for knocking her down with a tricycle. But be honest, it's always about money. And whoever says it's not is, well, lying. So, don't lie to yourself about it, either.

I'm not afraid. I'm not sure I could make a foul shot with the score tied and no time remaining. I get nervous—before picking a jury, taking a crucial deposition, arguing a simple motion. It passes quickly, but am I the only one? No one else admits to butterflies. That's why I love golf. After playing a round, you know everything about a person—who cheats, who chokes, and whose game is better in the bar than on the green.

Exaggeration abounds once you walk up those cold courthouse steps. So many promise verdicts but never seem to pick a jury.

I can wing it. I've seen it, done it all, I tell myself. This is mostly true—so why should I spend days preparing for a deposition, reading every document, memorizing the file. I'll ask a million questions and I'm bound to cover every issue. Well, almost. Because preparation is the difference between success and failure. No one can wing it. The superstars—Michael Jordan, LeBron, Peyton—practice as hard as they play. They're focused, determined individuals who work to be better. Sure, they're naturals, but their continual desire for excellence separates them from those who coast on talent alone. Unless you can dunk backwards, hit the books.

We're not telling the witness what to say. The woodshed. It's where, I guess, people once were taken for punishment. In those days, it meant a spanking or caning. Today, we apply the term *woodshedding* to the time we spend with our witnesses before their deposition or trial testimony.

Recently, a relatively unimportant witness was deposed and she admitted to 40 hours over six days of prep by her lawyers, including videotape so she could see how she appeared. Her actual deposition lasted only a day. I could predict which questions she'd answer, "I don't know" or "I don't remember." When lawyers say they haven't suggested testimony, they usually have. No witness can resist hour after hour of "suggested" responses. They learn the party line and parrot it. I don't have a solution, of course, except to say that any witness who is in the woodshed for more than a few hours is just not credible.

Well, it's more than they gave us. Thousands of documents are dumped in no particular order and not categorized. Without a judge ordering parties to produce in a timely, orderly fashion, chaos and mistrust result. We then respond in kind and the merry-go-round continues for years. Have we ever considered ethical practice as not only more efficient but more effective?

Integrity, always admirable, is occasionally difficult to maintain during litigation. In the quiet of your office, examine your strategy and your actions, and acknowledge if they are built on deception. Before you can be honest with your opponent, you must first be honest with yourself.

Screwing Up

I remember them all. The time I was too lazy to read 842 pages of the hospital record and, after the jury tossed me in the gutter, a smart-ass juror asked pointedly why I didn't mention the nurse's note hidden on page 496. Or when I left my expert's report on my desk and the judge, fat face filled with frustration, held out his hand for the document, and when I mumbled, "I can't find it," quickly and gleefully granted defendant's summary judgment motion. Or after my neighbor Mrs. Mullaney called, sobbing that she was knocked down by this gigantic, vicious dog—"He put his paws on my shoulders and now I have a broken hip and I have to get screws and plates." I started her lawsuit only to discover that the dog was one of those tiny Paris Hilton pets, weighing about the same as one of my chins.

And that's just the beginning. There are plenty more such slip-ups. Some only known to me and God, which you couldn't get me to disclose even if you made me listen to Joe Biden speeches all day. I haven't listed these blunders on my website or in the propaganda that sits neatly in our reception area. Yeah, there were times, too many of course, when I didn't study all precedent, didn't read every word of every document, didn't go over and over every possible question before my client, at his deposition, admitted he wasn't looking when he crossed the street.

171

Many lawyers only boast of their triumphs—their brilliance, insight, eloquence. They stalk jaded courthouse halls hunting for a slight smile or nod, ecstatic for a murmured, "How ya doin'?" so they can stop and harangue about their latest ploy, unctuous conceit spilling down striped red ties onto cheap shoes.

Not me. I make mistakes, lose cases, and don't win all the beauty contests. Clients, foolish and delusional, have fired my butt. Hey, one of my partners might read this, so I must add that these errors, these missteps have been infrequent, rare, hardly ever. After all, I've endured 30-plus years in this profession, and my successes, not all front-page material, have allowed me the privilege of paying myriad cell phone bills, outrageous car insurance premiums, and four tuitions at Boston College.

So I'm here to tell the truth, especially to the young'uns whose clear eyes and crisp smiles can't hide their anxiety, the concern that they're not clever enough, confident enough, or aggressive enough to please the partner, the firm, or themselves. At a recent football game, I ran into one of my daughter's friends who would soon start at a prestigious large firm, one that would have tossed my résumé in the trash. You'll be fine, I counseled. You'll do great. Her face was lined with disbelief and fear. But she will do well, because the fancy partners at her firm aren't perfect. You pull back the curtain and most are bright, hard-working, experienced litigators. But Clarence Darrow? Not even close.

Sure there are some lawyers so eloquent, so knowledgeable, so prepared that every moment of trial runs smoothly. But very few. Heck, I can't sit through most depositions because the questioning is convoluted, exhibits can't be located; there's no rhythm, no pace. Pure torture.

So get used to it—you're gonna screw up. And often. The flubs will be frequent when you start, little baby counselors sitting up straight, reading the file, paying attention. You'll miss typos, not cite a case, fail to adhere to the judge's rules—the list is endless. But do me a favor: Don't miss a statute, fail to plead or answer properly, or miss a deadline for a judge who actually enforces them. Try not to have your case dismissed. That'll cause nightmares that last, well, forever.

You learn through mistakes, or near disasters—or you should. Maybe you forget to move to dismiss an affirmative defense of improper service until a week before the statute runs, so you spend the next few days rushing about in an effort to reserve the defendant properly. Maybe you serve notice on the wrong municipal agency only to have the bored clerk growl, "Hey, shouldn't this go to the corporation counsel?" Each mistake is a lesson, and if you study the mistakes of others, you can accelerate your education. I used to read legal malpractice decisions not to revel in the misery of others (although sometimes an evil smile would creep to my lips) but to learn what errors to avoid.

So how do you prevent blunders, from overlooking a crucial case to having your expert barred from testifying? The answer is pretty simple: preparation and attention to detail. There's no substitute. Read all the documents, every stinking word. Today, papers are computer-produced: 50-page complaints appear in minutes, rogs and document requests in seconds. Despite the accelerating torrent of paper, you have to read it—all of it. Make sure your papers include what's required. Are all affirmative defenses listed? Were punitives pled properly? Every case is different, so don't rush; take a breath and think. Just because some form documents have been used religiously for the past decade doesn't mean they're perfect.

Ask for help, and recruit another set or two of eyes. Don't believe you're infallible. More importantly, don't be afraid to ask the simple, elementary questions. Does my argument make sense? What did I forget? Should I request other documents? Is this answer to rog number 987 correctly worded? Sure, some immature gasbag like me will brand you brainless for omitting an essential element of a claim. So what? Would you rather be summoned to a crowded corner office to hear the dreaded words, "I guess we have to notify our malpractice carrier."?

Check and double-check. Of course there's never enough time. Six assignments are due by day's end. But you have to check. Be forewarned. Every year a front-page story describes how a seemingly small typo brings the house down and causes agita. The prospectus listed September 1, 2008, as the date instead of 2009, which costs millions in damages, additional litigation fees, and malpractice premiums. Or when the amount of the mortgage was supposed to be $92,885,000 but a secretary omitted the zeros and $92,885 was repeated through the documents more than 100 times. Ouch!

Don't rely on others. Sure, the firm has a calendar system which tracks deadlines. Since I've never trusted a soul, I've kept my own as well. Heck, when I had to file an important document or interview a crucial witness, I did it myself. I'd ask the clerk a hundred questions just so I wouldn't wake up in the dark, pillow soaked with sweat. If necessary, jump on the subway, hop in your car, and do it yourself. Sure, it's easier to lounge in your office, but this is your livelihood, your life. You learn by doing, not by delegating.

I mocked my father when he told me I wouldn't know anything until I was 50. I'd arrogantly mouth the Dylan words: "Your sons and your daughters are beyond your command, your old road is rapidly agin'." My college friends and I knew how to end war, hunger, and discrimination. All before we were 21. Now that I comb gray hair, I appreciate my dad's wisdom. Experience is the best educator. Along the way, you'll take some body blows and sport the occasional black eye, but you'll survive wiser and more efficient.

Don't try to do what you don't know. I once agreed to aid a friend whose louse of a husband wanted a divorce. She moved back with Mom. No kids, no house, no real assets. Simple, right? Yes, until my client called one evening and advised that her husband was away and that she wanted to clean out the apartment. Was that okay? After I stopped mumbling and delaying, I admitted I had no clue, and she should immediately contact a colleague who specialized in this craziness.

Nothing in our business is easy. If it's beyond your knowledge and experience—no matter how lucrative—refer it out or co-counsel with another who has expertise. The quickest way to become a malpractice defendant yourself is to take a dog case believing a nasty letter or two will make everyone happy, only to realize that a suit must be filed, followed by numerous motions, depositions, and, sadly, a long, losing trial. Unreasonable clients—are there any other kind?—demand time, money, and patience. Eventually, you either ignore the dreaded file or neglect more significant, profitable work. One puts you in personal peril and the other makes you poorer.

I don't care if it's your mother-in-law. If it's not economically worth it, politely decline and provide a list of competent attorneys. The best cases are the ones you don't take. She'll never like you anyway.

So, when your face turns scarlet, when you assume you're the worst lawyer in the universe, when you're chewed out by some pompous pharaoh, remember that we all were there. We all mess up, even Derek Jeter. Relax, hang in there. You're never as good as you imagine, nor are you as bad as you believe.

Kentucky

It happened all the time. I would be walking to Starbucks on the silent sidewalks of Lexington to appease my addiction to all things New York with a purchase of *The New York Times*. Out of nowhere, a garbageman, or a young attractive office worker, or a guy who looked like he could use a long shower would look at me and happily declare, "Good morning."

"Whoa, whoa, what does he want?" was my initial internal reaction. My head swiveled like that kid in *The Exorcist* to make sure I wasn't being set up. It took a few seconds to process all this good cheer. Then I'd mumble a quick and quizzical "Good morning," with "Whats goin' on here?" running through my calloused brain. "Have a nice day, sir," would be the delighted response. I'd try to reply in the same sincere, happy tone, but I hadn't had coffee and my "good morning"s were at best limited to a nod of the head as I rushed to the office or court, and through life. "Yeah, you, too," is all I could mumble.

Whenever I exited the elevator at Stoll Keenon Ogden—a local Lexington law firm—Linda or Sarah, the receptionists, would always announce, "Good morning," with a smile no less. And what really blew me away was that even if I returned the smile and the "Good morning," it didn't end. It was like a whole conversation. I was actually expected to stop and talk to someone. In fact, not just someone, but everyone. And I had to ask about their day and wish them well. Pleeeeeeease. I wish everyone the best and always. But do I have to tell them? Guess what? In Kentucky, you do.

"Good morning."
"Good morning to you, Linda."
"And how are yew?" (At least that's how it sounded to me.)
"Fine, thank you, and how are you today?"
"Thank yew. I'm good. Now have a good day."
"I will and you, too, thank you."
"I hope so. You're welcome."
"Thank you."

It was limitless. A month of *thank yew*s before a stitch of work was done. More conversation than I had with my wife in 39 years. And you had to stop and look the person in the eye and smile. Eventually, I got it. *Good morning* wasn't the usual trite, meaningless phrase that we spit out as we rush to our desks or on the crowded midtown streets. Here in Kentucky, the South, it was a ritual of good manners and elegant taste. People actually wanted you to have a good day, wanted you to be happy, wanted you to smile. Boy, was this hard.

I finally figured a way to cope: I'd initiate the greetings. The sooner I started all this friendly chatter, the sooner it would end, I figured. I'd "Good morning" strangers on the street, cashiers, waitresses. And I'd try to smile and be pleasant. It took discipline and effort, but it became enjoyable, especially when I slipped in a "sir" or "ma'am." I even developed a slight drawl, which made my day, because I have always desperately craved an accent.

It took months to understand this place called Kentucky. I knew about Adolph Rupp and the runts and Jamaal Mashburn—from the Bronx—and the Duke game and all. And I had once ridden a horse in Prospect Park. I sure wasn't one of these snobby New Yorkers who thought all southerners were Gomer Pyles, because my father had traveled for work. He spent months in Baton Rouge and Texas, and always told us about the exciting Friday night high school football games and how the southern girls were the prettiest. Of course, I had been in the South, too—Chattanooga, Charleston, Savannah, Memphis, even South Jersey—so I thought I knew everything, knew enough to lie and to say that Sherman Street, where I was born and raised, was named after Roger Sherman—you know, the Great Compromiser, not that General William Tecumseh who marched to the sea.

But, like most New Yorkers who believe they know all but really know nothing, I was amazed to learn how little I knew of basic Southern amenities. To say "please" and "thank you," be respectful of elders, be nice, wish people well—that I knew, sort of. It was all the stuff my parents drilled into me. Heck, my dad used to tip his hat to women on the street. And, of course, I believed I was doing all these things, but I really wasn't.

And am I going to accept blame for allowing my manners to deteriorate? No way. I'll be a good Manhattan liberal and blame my environment—in this case, a lifetime of riding the F and R subway lines. Oh, it was fun in grammar school when the train left the dark, dirty tunnel and soared high above Brooklyn with impressive views of the city skyline, but that lasted about a week until I sat next to some guy who smelled worse than one of those thoroughbred stalls filled with manure.

Just riding the subway makes one callous. My daughter Lizzy told me about her ride on the "Happy Train." Some nut strolled into her subway car and announced, "Welcome to the Happy Train. This is the Happy Train," as he strutted around the car. "That's right, don't smile 'cause if you smile you'll be arrested by the 'Glum Police.'" He held a mirror in front of a passenger's face and sang, "Look at that beautiful person. Look at that beautiful face." Not only did he not want money, but he also asked two tough teens if they wanted a dollar. Eventually, people raised their eyes from their newspapers, looked at one another and smiled, which, I guess, was his point. That and the website he was advertising.

In New York, you're taught from infancy to show no emotion because there have to be a good hundred thousand certified lunatics in the Big Apple. And probably three or four times that amount are just a stray word or two from becoming homicidal maniacs. "You talkin' to me? You talkin' to me? You talkin' to me?" Everyone's a potential Travis Bickle.

In Kentucky, no one, it seems, received the same life lessons. That's not to say they don't have sharp elbows. When I first arrived in Lexington to represent families of victims of the Comair air crash tragedy, a meeting was held to form a plaintiffs' steering committee. The local lawyers didn't exactly meet the out-of-towners with Maker's Mark and burgoo. For some crazy reason, they distrusted us New Yorkers, Chicagoans, even those from Cincinnati. And they weren't afraid to tell us, albeit in a polite, refined manner. Even a soft drawl can't disguise the meaning of "jump in the lake" (or other four-letter words). Yeah, initially some didn't like us much. And that feeling was reinforced after the first court conference, when some of us Yankees would continually pop up to address the court. When finished, another would immediately jump up to agree, in hopes of attracting a TV camera or two. Reminded me a bit of that arcade game, Whac-a-Mole, where a child, holding a padded mallet, hits the mole every time one pops up. The faster the child hits the mole, the faster the next one pops up.

It took time, but slowly the local boys began to trust us national big shots. They eventually figured out that we weren't going to steal their thoroughbreds and turn them into carriage horses dragging tourists through Central Park. Those who practiced in Kentucky were talented lawyers and fine people who realized that there was enough work for all with the hundreds of thousands of discovery documents, myriad motions, depositions, and letters flying back and forth. What I learned was not only were they superb, diligent lawyers, but they were also better than most of us. And loads of fun to share a drink or meal, especially if University of Kentucky won that week—or lost, if they were from Louisville.

Even our adversaries were palatable, played fewer games, were more open and credible than I was used to. Don't get me wrong: If the Pope were across the table at a deposition and told me he produced all relevant documents, I would suggest he immediately go to confession. For the most part, however, our opponents were professional, and the typical rancor and lectures during depositions were minimal. And the presiding judge, Senior Judge Karl S. Forester, was about as good as it gets. Intelligent and fair, he managed this case with dignity and soft-spoken steel.

So I came to enjoy, actually like, the measured rhythm of daily life. I marveled at the magnificent horse farms, rolling hills, and fields of bluegrass, which, let's be honest, look green. I most enjoyed the people; nature is nice and all, but after five minutes, picturesque landscape and stately thoroughbreds are pretty boring. Yet Kentucky isn't perfect. Downtown lunch joints close whenever, no later than 3 P.M., and the pizza leaves something to be desired.

Yet my education wasn't limited to civility and when to buy a tuna melt. Chilling reminders of Lexington's role in the slave trade exist. Whenever I passed the old Fayette County Courthouse, I would read the plaques noting that at Cheapside, slaves were sold, children separated from their families. As a father of four, I would visualize the horror of being shackled and losing not only freedom but also your children. This stain on our national soul is more visible in the South. Only the discovery of an African burial ground near the courts in downtown Manhattan caused me to realize that slavery existed and thrived in New York for 200 years, until 1827.

I don't think I could ever live in Kentucky. I'm just not used to having that many people use English as their primary language. And it's way too easy to park. But it was an honor to represent good and honest people, to litigate with intelligent and hard-working attorneys, and to learn something about America and myself.

Saints

Like pilgrims approaching Lourdes, clients trek into our imposing offices searching for a cure. They arrive when disaster or disgrace loom, hopeful that our words, our wisdom will provide healing. Through our guidance, we remove this burden and make it our own. We insist that clients follow our direction, for if they do, the gloom that envelops their life, their business will surely become bright, soothing light.

Rarely during contested litigation do we seek our clients' advice, consult with them on strategy. We are the professionals, after all. They are civilians—uneducated in law, procedure, trial. During these intense battles, we concentrate on discovery, depositions, the latest appellate court ruling. Clients are ignored, for we have a motion on and we must persuade the judge to rule in our favor.

On occasion after a case ends and the file is closed, I hear a sound, glance at an image, and former clients come to mind. I remember those I represented and wonder whatever happened. In those too rare moments of reflection, I realize that some clients radiated goodness and generosity. They endured the horrifying accident, the unexpected death, the endless suffering with grace and resolve. During the lawsuit, I was too frenzied, too focused on winning. Yet now that these clients are but a distant memory, I realize how much they taught, not through posturing or bombast, but through quiet acts of heroism.

This is one such story.

Shortly after I was admitted to the bar in 1978, a classmate, Eddie Lopez, referred his cousin, Mrs. Gonzalez, who believed that her daughter's severe disability was caused by the doctor's negligence during birth. I interviewed the family, obtained the medical records, and sat with a nurse who guided me through the labor and delivery chart. We hired experts, who agreed with the validity of the claim. After a few years of contentious litigation and with a jury in the box, we settled. My first million-dollar win.

As soon as the stipulation of settlement was placed on the record, the partner trying the case disappeared. I searched the courthouse until he eventually reappeared and mumbled something about the bathroom. The next day, as I thumbed through *The Daily News*, I saw an article about the Gonzalez settlement, with a picture of our clients. A similar article appeared in *The New York Post*. The partner merely shook his head and laughed when I asked how the press learned of our victory.

As a result, our office was deluged with calls from families with similar handicapped children. This was the early 1980s, before obstetrical medical malpractice became a full-blown specialty. In addition, in those ancient times, the New York statute of limitations for infants began when the child turned 18 and ran to age 21, so the pool of potential plaintiffs was large.

I visited many a home, sat on couches with plastic slipcovers, heard about the lengthy labors, doctors arriving at the hospital late, the mother ignored for hours until a frenzied forceps delivery with doctors shouting orders and a nurse rushing with the newborn to the neonatal intensive care unit. So I learned obstetrics—the techniques of delivering a baby, how to read fetal monitoring strips, and the signs of fetal distress. One case involved the Ryan family, whose son was a teen when they came to see me sometime in 1983.

The Ryans were from the West Indies, with proper manners and dress, along with lilting accents that I had trouble understanding since I was used to the universally acclaimed language known as Brooklynese. Like most immigrants, Mr. Ryan worked two jobs while his wife remained home to care for their five children, including their severely handicapped son. Johnny couldn't talk or walk, but that didn't deter the Ryans from providing unconditional love and care.

I first met Johnny when I climbed the stairs of the family's small brick walk-up in a crime-ridden, mostly burned-out neighborhood. Johnny was 16 and large, sitting in his wheelchair. Whenever I first met a child like Johnny with twisted limbs and spastic movements, my initial reaction, truthfully, was one of selfishness. Yes, my heart ached for the child and drove my determination to help the family. But I was secretly relieved that this burden was theirs, not mine. Evil thoughts would slither into my mind: Maybe it would have been better had these children—images of God—never survived the botched deliveries. I hated these feelings and vowed to banish them from darkening my soul, but they stubbornly returned whenever I sat in a similar living room taking notes and glancing at a child who will never sing a nursery rhyme.

By the time I was contacted by Mr. Ryan, I was proficient at evaluating the merits of the claim. So I went through my routine of obtaining records, consulting experts, including a pediatric neurologist who would examine the youngster to detail damages and to solidify causation. These exams occurred at the doctor's office on Long Island, so I would pick up my clients at their home, pile into my car, and drive to the suburbs.

Johnny was nearly fully grown, and getting him up and down the narrow tenement stairs was not easy. Mr. Ryan's solution was to carry him by placing him over his shoulder like the proverbial sack of potatoes. Whenever Johnny left the apartment—to the doctors, to the store, to sit on the stoop in the sun—Mr. Ryan, not a large man, lifted his son and his 140 pounds onto his shoulder and labored up and down those many steps. All without complaint and with inherent cheerfulness.

We litigated Johnny's case against an experienced defense lawyer. If he had money, he would tell you, and if it was within his authority, he would settle. If you wanted a dollar more, he would try it. No bravado, no lengthy negotiations. After a deposition, he told me he could make an offer, and, in 1986, we settled. With part of the proceeds, we structured the settlement so the Ryan family would receive a monthly stipend for the rest of Johnny's life to ensure that funds would always be available for his care.

Happy with the result, I immediately turned to other cases, my young family, and the maelstrom that made those years pass much too quickly. I heard from the Ryan family once or twice over the many years. The structured payments were overseen by the Guardian Department in the bureaucratic Surrogate's Court, and periodically issues with access to the funds arose, which I assigned to those more patient in my office (which was everyone).

I recently received a call from Mr. Ryan telling me in a grieving voice that Johnny had died. With an estate to open, I met with Mr. Ryan and some of his children. Mr. Ryan was older now, but still in shirt and tie; his sadness and that of his children was palpable. I had expected words of sorrow, but also a flicker of relief—that after 44 years, the family would take comfort in God's goodness and be grateful that their burden of caring—all day, every day—for Johnny was over. There was none of this heartless sentiment.

"Johnny was a blessing, Mr. Nolan. A blessing," said one sister as the others nodded in agreement. "He was." This was from a woman who devoted her life to her brother, caring for him—along with her parents—since she was in her teens. This was her vocation, her only job ever. Her daily existence was to love and look after her brother. She didn't have a cell phone, wasn't on Facebook, and didn't need a Prada purse.

"The doctor said that people like Johnny usually don't live this long. But he did because we took such good care of him," she added proudly. And now she will continue her works of mercy by taking care of her parents who are now in their 80s. But not alone. Her siblings will be there as well, even the grandchildren who have the same Ryan DNA—generosity and love.

I was ashamed, of course, of my cynicism, my weakness. I only saw sacrifice while they saw humanity. They eagerly showed me Johnny's small room and the lift which was used to get him in and out of bed. "Wasn't he so handsome?" they remarked as they pointed to his photo. They said that he made them happy when he would reach and hug them if they sat close to him. He made them laugh when he would slap their hand away if he didn't want something. I saw a wheelchair; they saw a person, with dignity and worth.

They never complained about life's unfairness during the litigation 25 years ago and didn't complain now, except to state that

Johnny was taken much too soon. They will miss their son, their brother, their blessing.

In a world of war, hatred, and suffering, goodness exists. It may be difficult to notice as we focus on the material, on the celebrated. But goodness is there, often silent, often hidden. It's on bucolic family farms and rough streets of inner cities. Look for it, find it, practice it. It will change your life.

The Life

I never wanted to be a lawyer. No one else in the neighborhood dreamed of being the next Clarence Darrow or arguing before the Supreme Court. Joe Kelly wanted to be Ernie Banks. Joey Hajjar dreamed of roaming center field in Yankee Stadium like the Mick. As a short, skinny kid, I wanted to dribble through a crowd and wow them like Cousy.

Joe Kelly delivered mail and the Haj owned a pool business in Austin. I became a lawyer and it's not so bad. Of course, I would still like to be Dwyane Wade throwing the no-look pass to LeBron. Or making a three at the buzzer to finish the Lakers. Maybe in my next life.

But I'm tired of all the whining and moaning, as if legal work were the current equivalent of scraping coal out of the dust-encrusted mines of the 1930s. Step back and take an objective look at lawyer gripes: Isn't it terrible that our lofty profession—which once consisted of gentlemen whose word was sacred—has degenerated into a business where adjournments of minor matters must be in writing with affidavits? I can't browse a legal publication without an old windbag (like me) lamenting the loss of camaraderie, or some judge in her black robes, who hasn't bought a meal since ascending her throne, decrying the loss of courtesy. Or some wide-eyed, Generation-X, spoiled suburbanite with an expensive Ivy League education wailing that the legal profession doesn't do enough for the poor. And, by the way, that six-figure salary just isn't enough to pay back those student loans and a trip to Aspen.

We act like the profession should and can be perfect. We want to be loved and respected by the public. We are indignant when one of our own steals, cheats, or even acts rudely. So what should we do? Legislate rules to compel our legions of colleagues to act like Mother Teresa? We seek an ideal that doesn't exist, and probably never existed. I was always taught that we are born imperfect and subject to temptation. And in my world, even my guardian angel loses an occasional struggle with Satan.

If I had always wanted to be treated with respect, I would have been a bartender—or changed my name and joined the Gambino crime family. If I really wanted to dedicate my life to others, I would still be teaching English in John Jay High School in Brooklyn, or I would have joined the Jesuits and worked with the peasants in Guatemala. And I don't mind another lawyer cursing me out occasionally. I've been called worse and by those who love me.

Let's face it. Law is a business—a huge, demanding business. But it's a good one, and we should be proud, most of the time. It's work and we struggle through it. Occasionally, however, we do good—help the widow, change the unjust law, or even aid the multinational corporation. Of course, we think of fees. But I have met only a few people who aren't concerned with money, and they usually wear clerical garb and take the vow of poverty. As a profession, we are better than most. As a lawyer unable to tell the truth, Jim Carrey was hilarious in *Liar Liar*, but he's a caricature. Don't be afraid to laugh at lawyer jokes—most are pretty funny—but they don't depict the whole profession.

So what are we? Huge firms with hundreds of lawyers, offices around the world, millions in revenues, partners working crazy hours with pressures enough to drive anyone to a third martini. And like any business, there must be profits and advertising and tough decisions based not on personality but on productivity. Who didn't know this when he started law school?

Of course, I wish it could be different. Maybe it once was. Once, perhaps, friendship was valued above money, courtesy was the norm, and summer vacations actually existed. But that isn't the real world of today, in any profession. Ask Jeff Immelt of GE or Alan Mullaly of Ford if they have pressures. Ask if they work weekends or ever fired a friend. Ask them how often they sleep through a night.

In my Brooklyn neighborhood, I was taught that work was good. If you wanted to buy something, you had to work. Your parents worried about making it from paycheck to paycheck, never mind the baseball glove. So we had paper routes or delivered groceries or sold popcorn in the Prospect Park zoo. Nothing was owed and nothing was given to you. If you wanted it, you earned it. And you had to work at everything, including education and sports. And sometimes, no matter how hard you worked, another would get a better grade or make the crucial jump shot.

So it is with lawyers. The interminable hours spent studying IRS regulations don't entitle you to success. And don't equate the horrific law school years with the three and a half years my father spent in Africa and Europe fighting World War II or the time my partner Gerry Lear spent in Vietnam piloting helicopters. With a modicum of luck, those with some intelligence who work diligently will succeed. Yet, on occasion, another less-deserving lawyer will win the case, become partner, be lauded on the legal blogs. Life is unfair, as Jack Kennedy once noted. And his death proved he was correct.

Yes, law is work—hard, monotonous, challenging work. Accept it and stop complaining. Keep it in perspective. Compare your work to a cop's, or a factory worker's, or my wife's job as a teacher and mother of four. Sadly, most of the moaning seems to come from men, not from those lawyers who are also mothers, whose days begin when they arrive home. We shouldn't have to work so hard. We should make a ton of money without having to stay in the office past six. Too often we sound like, well, spoiled brats.

We work in offices and deal with people and paper. The only calluses on my hands are from holding my golf clubs too tightly. We're not on the street chasing some low-life scum whacked out on drugs who wouldn't mind putting a bullet in your face. We're not welding thousands of the same doors on Toyotas, dreaming daily of Florida retirement to escape the monotony that crushes the spirit. And the fire-fighters, farm workers, and waiters will never earn the

$100,000-plus that the first-year associates make at the white-shoe firms. Ask your cleaning woman if she would work 80 hours a week to earn $75,000. The truth is, she probably works harder for much less. And that you have a cleaning woman speaks volumes. Don't be afraid to count your blessings.

There are other careers. Law is a grind and not the best choice for all. Just because your mother introduces you as a "big-shot lawyer" doesn't mean you're a failure if you give up the big bucks for journalism, art, or raising children.

I am sure there was a time when it was different—when a handshake was all that was necessary. A written contract was superfluous. Still, after 34 years of practice, I find that another lawyer's word is usually sufficient for an adjournment, or to settle the case. It is rare that I have been screwed by one who lies and cheats. Sure, I want all agreements memorialized, but I'm a paranoid New Yorker. And why is that so bad? Was it really that much better years ago? Most attorneys can be trusted. Most are honorable. A few are snakes and a few will serve papers Christmas Eve. Put such behavior in the memory bank and remind them of it when they need a favor.

Sure, I've acted rudely, made a young lawyer cry at a deposition, and driven a few judges ballistic. And I've done some things that I dare not reveal except in the confessional and would rather forget. For those things, I'm ashamed. As I age, such idiocies lessen, but they may happen again. I'm far from perfect; ask my partners. But most of the time, I try to treat people fairly. And, almost always, I'm treated with courtesy by my adversaries.

Even most judges will accommodate your schedule. Sure, a few are bitter, power-mad egomaniacs who revel in making your life miserable. Others are partially corrupt or dumb as a bowling ball. But what occupation is exempt from such individuals? Most judges try to do the right thing. They run an imperfect system imperfectly, but 90 percent of the time it works. Only the exceptions are heralded in the media.

I'm not a big fan of advertising. I would prefer that reputation and experience determine who is retained. But even Muhammad Ali had to tell everyone that he was the greatest. So we have firm brochures, and newsletters, and copies of newspaper articles. Again, most are tastefully done. The public, however, only sees the billboard with the car wreck and the 1-800-Get-Rich telephone number. I, too, would rather not have my nonlawyer friends snicker when the crass ads are viewed, but I don't accept those as a reflection on me or my profession. I know better.

Our problem is that we do not communicate the good we do. We're like the 10 o'clock news—only crime, disaster, and tragedy are broadcast. Our countless works of mercy are ignored. In this, the organized bar is partly to blame. Its leaders are forever forming task forces to deal with misconduct, discovery abuse, or incivility. Or they pass resolutions to compel diversity, continuing legal education, or pro bono activity, as if we were ignorant, racist paparazzi who wouldn't lift a hand to aid another unless there was a $100 bill attached. I realize that we lawyers should always strive for perfection. I also realize that that's not going to happen: Some of my friends have been disbarred.

But let's celebrate our accomplishments. At least occasionally. I have made good and loyal friends. I have supported my family. I have been intellectually challenged. I have won and lost. I have done good and not so good. I never planned on being a lawyer, but I'm glad I am.

Index

About the Author

Kenneth P. Nolan specializes in personal injury and wrongful death litigation. He has tried a variety of cases—aviation, medical malpractice, construction, automobile, contract—in both state and federal court throughout the country. He has litigated many aviation disasters, including the Korean Air shootdown in 1983, the USAir Flight 5050 crash at LaGuardia in 1989, the TWA Flight 800 explosion in 1996, the Egyptair crash of 1999, the American Air Flight 587 disaster in Queens in 2001, the Comair accident in Lexington, Kentucky, in 2006, and the Colgan Air crash near Buffalo in 2009. He also represented 130 families who suffered losses from the Sept. 11, 2001, attacks before the Victim Compensation Fund and in actions against the terrorists and their supporters.

A lifelong resident of Brooklyn, Ken graduated from Brooklyn Law School in 1977. A writer and an advocate, he has written and was an editor for *The New York Times*. He is past editor-in-chief of *Litigation*, published by the ABA, and is now senior editor of and authors the "Sidebar" column. He was a member of the editorial board of the *ABA Journal* and *The New York State Bar Journal*. He has published legal articles on aviation law, personal injury, and trial techniques. He has lectured extensively throughout the United States and in England, France, Mexico, Canada, and Austria.

Ken and his wife, Nancy, have four children, Kenny, Caitlin, Elizabeth, and Claire, and one grandson, Luke. They live in Brooklyn and Shelter Island, New York.